THE

# SPHERE AND DUTIES

OF

# GOVERNMENT.

Translated from the German of

BARON WILHELM VON HUMBOLDT,

BY

JOSEPH COULTHARD, Jun.

" Le difficile est de ne promulguer que des lois nécessaires, de rester à jamais
fidèle à ce principe vraiment constitutionnel de la société, de se mettre en garde
contre la fureur de gouverner, la plus funeste maladie des gouvernemens modernes."—MIRABEAU *l'Aîné, sur l'Education Publique, p.* 69.

Martino Publishing
Mansfield Centre, CT
2014

*Martino Publishing*
*P.O. Box 373,*
*Mansfield Centre, CT 06250 USA*


ISBN    978-1-61427-713-2


© *2014  Martino Publishing*

Cover design by T. Matarazzo

*Printed in the United States of America On 100% Acid-Free Paper*

# THE

# SPHERE AND DUTIES

OF

# GOVERNMENT.

Translated from the German of

## BARON WILHELM VON HUMBOLDT,

BY

## JOSEPH COULTHARD, Jun.

" Le difficile est de ne promulguer que des lois nécessaires, de rester à jamais fidèle à ce principe vraiment constitutionnel de la société, de se mettre en garde contre la fureur de gouverner, la plus funeste maladie des gouvernemens modernes."—MIRABEAU *l'Aîné, sur l'Education Publique, p.* 69.

LONDON:

JOHN CHAPMAN,

8, KING WILLIAM STREET, STRAND.

MDCCCLIV.

# PREFACE.

THE book of which a translation is here offered to the English reader was published posthumously at Berlin, in the year 1852, by the Author's younger brother, Alexander von Humboldt, the eminent Naturalist. It appeared under the title of 'Ideen zu einem Versuch, die Gränzen der Wirksamkeit des Staats zu bestimmen;' forming part of the seventh and concluding volume of the 'Gesammelte Werke' of its distinguished author. Written in 1791, in his early manhood, and at a time when the ideas which it unfolds were in striking contrast to the events and opinions of the day, the book was long obnoxious to the scruples of the German Censorship; and his friend Schiller, who took much interest in its publication, had some difficulty in finding a publisher willing to incur the necessary responsibility. The Author therefore retained the manuscript in his possession, revising it from time to time, and re-writing considerable portions, which appeared in Schiller's 'Thalia' and the 'Berlin Monthly Review;' but, although the obstacles which at first opposed the issue of the book were subsequently removed, it was never given to the

world in a complete form during his life.  It is probable
that his important official engagements,* and those profound studies in critical philology, of which we have such
noble and enduring monuments in the literature of Ger-
many, left him no leisure to revert to this the chosen subject of his earlier labours.  But we cannot but feel grateful
to his distinguished brother, for giving publicity to a treatise which has such strong claims to attention, whether we
regard the eminence of its Author as a philosopher and a
statesman, the intrinsic value of its contents, or their peculiar interest at a time when the Sphere of Government seems
more than ever to require careful definition.  To English-

---

* In 1790 Humboldt was appointed a Councillor of Legation, and attached
to the High Court of Berlin.  In 1791 he resigned these offices, and the next
ten years of his life (during which the present work was written) were spent
in travel, literary activity, and constant intercourse with Goethe, Schiller,
Wolf, etc.  In 1802 he was made Privy Councillor of Legation and Ambassador at the Papal Court, in which capacity he resided six years at Rome.  On
giving up his diplomatic engagements, he was appointed in 1808 Privy Councillor of State; and as Minister of Worship and Public Instruction, was one of
the most active members of the Prussian Reform Ministry, until, through the
influence of Napoleon, it was dismissed in 1810.  Among many other important improvements and reforms, he founded the University of Berlin.  Soon
after, he was appointed Ambassador and Plenipotentiary at the Austrian Court,
with the additional title of Privy Minister of State.  In 1813 he was Plenipotentiary at the Peace Congress of Prague, at Chatillon, and subsequently at
the Congress of Vienna.  He afterwards visited Paris in a diplomatic capacity; and it was here that Madame de Staël was so much impressed with his
genius and culture, that she called him " la plus grande capacité de l'Europe."
In 1818 he was appointed to the Ministry of the Interior; but his strenuous
advocacy of constitutional liberty (in opposition to the Carlsbad decrees) was
an insuperable obstacle to the schemes of the Cabinets of Vienna and Peters-
burg, and of some of his colleagues in the Ministry of Prussia.  He was
offered the ministerial pension of 6000 dollars, but, refusing it, retired to
prosecute his more congenial literary labours.

men, least of all, is it likely to prove unattractive or unin-
structive, since it endeavours to show the theoretical ideal
of a policy to which their institutions have made a gradual
and instinctive approximation; and contributes important
ideas towards the solution of questions which now lie so
near to the heart and conscience of the English public.

With respect to the translation, I have aimed at scrupu-
lous fidelity; believing that, even where there may be some
obscurity (as in one or two of the earlier chapters), the in-
telligent reader would prefer the *ipsissima verba* of so great
a man, to any arbitrary construction put upon them by his
translator.  Still, I have spared no pains to discover the
author's sense in all cases, and to give it in simple and unmistakable words; and I would here mention, with grateful
acknowledgment, the valuable assistance I have received in
this endeavour from my accomplished German friend, Mr.
Eugen Oswald: those who are best acquainted with the
peculiarities of thought and style which characterize the
writer, will be best able to appreciate the importance of such
assistance.

In conclusion, I cannot but feel that there may be many to
whom this book contains little to recommend itself;—little
of showy paradox or high-sounding declamation, little of
piquant attack or unhesitating dogmatism, little immediate
reference to sects, or parties, or political schools; but I would
also venture to anticipate that there are others, to whom
the subject is no less congenial, who would willingly listen
to a calm investigation of the most important questions that

can occupy the attention of the statesman and the moralist, to earnest ideas clothed in simple and well-measured words; and that these will receive with welcome any worthy contribution to the expanding opinions of our day and nation, and look in these "Ideas," perhaps not unsuccessfully, for some true and abiding materials towards the structure of some fairer polity of the future.

BRAMPTON,
*August 4th,* 1854.

\*\*\* In the MS. of the Third Chapter, on "Positive Welfare," there occurs an hiatus of a few pages. This has not been supplied in the German edition, published by the Author's brother; but the thread of the argument is sufficiently clear, from the Author's summary, to occasion little difficulty to the reader in continuing it in his own mind.

# CONTENTS.

—◆—

## CHAPTER I.

Object of the Inquiry defined.—An Inquiry seldom prosecuted, though of the highest importance.—Historical View of the limits which States have practically assigned to their sphere of action.—Difference between Ancient and Modern States.—On the Aim of the State Organization in general.—Should the Solicitude of the State be confined to the preservation of SECURITY, or should it attempt to provide for the POSITIVE WELFARE of the Nation ?—Legislators and Authors in favour of the latter opinion.—Notwithstanding their conclusions, this question seems to require a profounder Investigation.—This Investigation can proceed only from a consideration of Human Nature and its highest aims.

## CHAPTER II.

Man's highest end is the highest and most harmonious Development of his Powers in their perfect Individuality.—Conditions necessary for the attainment of this end: Freedom of Action and a Variety of Situations.—Closer application of these positions to the inner life of man.—Historical confirmation.—Highest Principle of the whole Inquiry derived from these considerations.

# CHAPTER III.

Scope of this Chapter.—A Solicitude of the State for the Positive
Welfare of the Citizen is hurtful.—For it creates uniformity;
weakens the power and resources of the nation; confuses and
impedes the reaction even of mere corporeal pursuits, and of external relations in general, on the human mind and character;
must operate upon a promiscuous mass of individuals, and
therefore does harm to these by measures which cannot meet
individual cases; it hinders the development of individuality
in human nature; it increases the difficulty of administration,
multiplies the means necessary for it, and so becomes a source
of manifold evils; lastly, it tends to confound the just and natural points of view from which men are accustomed to regard
the most important objects.—Vindication from the Charge of
having overdrawn these evils.—Advantages of an opposite System.—General Principle.—Means of a State Solicitude directed
to the Positive Welfare of the Citizen.—Their pernicious character.—Difference between the accomplishment of any object
by the State in its capacity of State, and the same effected by
the efforts of the Citizens.—Examination of the objection, that
a Solicitude of the State for the Positive Welfare of the Citizen
is necessary, because it might not be possible without it to obtain the same external ends, and realize the same essential results.—This shown to be possible, especially in the common
Associations of the Citizens under their voluntary management.—This voluntary management superior to State arrangements.

# CHAPTER IV.

This Solicitude is necessary: it constitutes the real end of the State.
—General Principle: confirmed by History.

*b*

# SPHERE AND DUTIES OF GOVERNMENT.

## CHAPTER I.

### INTRODUCTION.

To discover the legitimate objects to which the energies of
State organizations should be directed, and define the limits
within which those energies should be exercised, is the design of the following pages. That the solution of this prime
question of political philosophy must be pregnant with interest and high practical importance is sufficiently evident;
and if we compare the most remarkable political constitutions with each other, and with the opinions of the most
eminent philosophers, we shall, with reason, be surprised to
find it so insufficiently discussed and vaguely answered; and
agree, that any attempt to prosecute the inquiry with more
success, is far from being a vain and superfluous labour.

Those who have either themselves remodelled the frame-
work of State constitutions, or proposed schemes of political
reform, seem mostly to have studied how to apportion the
respective provinces which the nation, and any of its separate
elements, should justly share in the administration,—to assign the due functions of each in the governmental plan,
—and to adopt the precautions necessary for preserving the
integrity of the several interests at stake. But in every

B

attempt to frame or reorganize a political constitution, there
are two grand objects, it seems to me, to be distinctly kept
in view, neither of which can be overlooked or made subordinate without serious injury to the common design; these
are—first, to determine, as regards the nation in question,
who shall govern, who shall be governed, and to arrange
the actual working of the constituted power; and secondly,
to prescribe the exact sphere to which the government,
once constructed, should extend or confine its operations.
The latter object, which more immediately embraces the private life of the citizen, and more especially determines the
limits of his free, spontaneous activity, is, strictly speaking,
the true ultimate purpose; the former is only a necessary
means for arriving at this important end.  And yet, however strange it may appear, it is to the attainment of the
first of these ends that man directs his most earnest attention; and, as it becomes us to show, this exclusive pursuit
of one definite purpose only coincides with the usual manifestation of human activity.  It is in the prosecution of some
single object, and in striving to reach its accomplishment by
the combined application of his moral and physical energies,
that the true happiness of man, in his full vigour and development, consists.  Possession, it is true, crowns exertion
with repose; but it is only in the illusions of fancy that it
has power to charm our eyes.  If we consider the position
of man in the universe,—if we remember the constant tendency of his energies towards some definite activity, and recognize the influence of surrounding nature, which is ever
provoking him to exertion, we shall be ready to acknowledge that repose and possession do not indeed exist but in
imagination.  Now the partial or one-sided man finds repose in the discontinuance of one line of action; and in him
whose powers are wholly undeveloped, one single object
only serves to elicit a few manifestations of energy.  It may

be well to observe, before deriving inferences from these general considerations on the usual tendency of man's activity, that the dissatisfaction we notice as attendant on possession, does not at all apply to that ideal of human perfection which is conceivable by imagination; but it is true, in the fullest sense, of the wholly uncultured man, and proportionately true of every intermediate gradation between this utter want of culture and that ideal standard above mentioned. It would appear then, from these general characteristics of human nature, that to the conqueror his triumph affords a more exquisite sense of enjoyment than the actual occupation of the territory he has won, and that the perilous commotion of reformation itself is dearer to the reformer than the calm enjoyment of the fruits which crown its successful issue. And thus it is true, in general, that the exercise of dominion has something in it more immediately agreeable to human nature than the mere reposeful sense of freedom; or, at least, that the solicitude to secure freedom is a dearer satisfaction than that which is afforded by its actual possession. Freedom is but the *possibility* of a various and indefinite activity; while government, or the exercise of dominion, is a single, but yet *real* activity. The ardent desire for freedom, therefore, is at first only too frequently suggested by the deep-felt consciousness of its absence.

But whatever the natural course of political development may be, and whatever the relation between the desire for freedom and the excessive tendency to governmental activity, it is still evident that the inquiry into the proper aims and limits of State agency must be of the highest importance — nay, that it is perhaps more vitally momentous than any other political question. That such an investigation comprises the ultimate object of all political science, has been already pointed out; but it is a truth that admits also of extensive practical application. Real State revolutions, or fresh organizations of the governing power, are always attended in their progress with many concurrent and fortuitous circumstances, and necessarily entail more or less injury to different interests; whereas a sovereign power that is actually existing—whether it be democratic, aristocratic, or monarchical—can extend or restrict its sphere of action in silence and secresy, and, in general, attains its ends more surely, in proportion as it avoids startling innovations. Those processes of human agency advance most happily to their consummation, which most faithfully resemble the operations of the natural world. The tiny seed, for example, which drops into the awaiting soil, unseen and unheeded, brings forth a far richer and more genial blessing in its growth and germination than the violent eruption of a volcano, which, however necessary, is always attended with destruction; and, if we justly pride ourselves on our superior culture and enlightenment, there is no other system of reform so happily adapted, by its spirit of calm and consistent progression, to the capacities and requirements of our own times.

It may easily be foreseen, therefore, that the important inquiry into the due limits of State agency must conduct us to an ampler range of freedom for human forces, and a richer diversity of circumstances and situations. Now the possibility of any higher degree of freedom presupposes a proportionate advancement in civilization,—a decreasing necessity of acting in large, compacted masses,—a richer variety of resources in the individual agents. If, then, the present age in reality possesses this increased culture and this power and diversity of resources, the freedom of which these are the precious conditions should unquestionably be accorded it. And so its methods of reform would be happily correspondent with a progressive civilization—if we do not err in supposing this to be its favourable characteristic. Generally speaking, it is the drawn sword of the nation which checks and overawes the physical strength of its rulers; but in our case, culture and enlightenment serve no less effectually to sway their thoughts and subdue their will, so that the actual concessions of reform seem rather ascribable to them than to the nation. If even to behold a people breaking their fetters asunder, in the full consciousness of their rights as men and citizens, is a beautiful and ennobling spectacle: it must be still more fair, and full of uplifting hope, to witness a prince himself unloosing the bonds of thraldom and granting freedom to his people,—nor this as the mere bounty of his gracious condescension, but as the discharge of his first and most indispensable duty; for it is nobler to see an object effected through a reverent regard for law and order, than conceded to the imperious demands of absolute necessity; and the more so, when we consider that the freedom which a nation strives to attain through the overthrow of existing institutions, is but as hope to enjoyment, as preparation to perfection, when compared with that which a State, once constituted, can bestow.

If we cast a glance at the history of political organizations, we shall find it difficult to decide, in the case of any one of them, the exact limits to which its activity was conformed, because we discover in none the systematic working out of any deliberate scheme, grounded on a certain basis of principle. We shall observe, that the freedom of the citizen has been limited from two points of view; that is, either from the necessity of organizing or securing the constitution, or from the expediency of providing for the moral and physical condition of the nation. These considerations have prevailed alternately, according as the constitution, in itself powerful, has required additional support, or as the views of the legislators have been more or less expanded. Often indeed both of these causes may be found operating conjointly. In the ancient States, almost all the institutions relating to the private life of the citizens were of a strictly political character. Possessed, as it was, of but little absolute authority, the constitution was mainly dependent for its duration on the will of the nation, and hence it was necessary to discover or propose means by which due harmony might be preserved between the character of established institutions and this tendency of national feeling. The same policy is still observable in small republican States; and if we were to regard it in the light of these circumstances alone, we might accept it as true, that the freedom of private life always increases in exact proportion as public freedom declines; whereas security always keeps pace with the latter. It is true the ancient legislators very often, and the ancient philosophers invariably, directed their attention to the inner life of the individual; and, in their eyes, the moral worth of human nature seemed to deserve the highest regard: of this we have an illustration in Plato's Republic, of which Rousseau has very truly observed that it has more the character of an educational than a political treatise. Now if we compare the example of the most modern States, with regard to this tendency, we shall find the design of acting for the individual citizen, and of providing for his welfare, to be clear and unmistakable from the number of laws and institutions directed to this end, and which often give a very determinate form to private life. The superior internal consistency of our constitutions,—their greater independence of national character and feeling,—the deeper influence of mere thinkers, who are naturally disposed to more expanded views,—the multitude of inventions which teach us to follow out and improve the common objects of national activity; and lastly, and before all, certain ideas of religion which represent the governing power as responsible, to a certain extent, for the moral and future welfare of the citizens, have all contributed to introduce this change and develope this positive solicitude. But if we examine into the origin of particular institutions and police-laws, we find that they frequently originate in the real or pretended necessity of imposing taxes on the subject, and in this we may trace the example, it is true, to the political characteristics of the ancient States, inasmuch as such institutions grow out of the same desire of securing the constitution which we noticed in them. With respect to those limitations of freedom, however, which do not so much affect the State as the individuals who compose it, we are led to notice a vast difference between ancient and modern governments. The ancients devoted their attention more exclusively to the harmonious development of the individual man, as man; the moderns are chiefly solicitous about his comfort, his prosperity, his productiveness. The former looked to virtue; the latter seek for happiness. And hence it follows, that the restrictions imposed on freedom in the ancient States were, in some important respects, more oppressive and dangerous than those which characterize our times. For they directly attacked that inner life of the soul, in which the individuality of human being essentially consists; and hence all the ancient nations betray a character of uniformity, which is not so much to be attributed to their want of higher refinement and more limited intercommunication, as to the systematic education of their youth in common (almost universal among them), and the designedly collective life of the citizens. But, in another point of view, it will be allowed that these ancient institutions contributed especially to preserve and elevate the vigorous activity of the individual man. The very desire which still animated all their political efforts, to train up temperate and nobleminded citizens, imparted a higher impulse to their whole spirit and character. With us, it is true, man is individually less restricted; but the influence of surrounding circumstances only the more operates to produce and continue a limiting agency,—a position, however, which does not preclude the possibility of beginning a conflict against these external hindrances, with our own internal antagonistic strength. And yet the peculiar nature of the limitations imposed on freedom in our States; the fact that they regard rather what man possesses than what he really is, and that with respect to the latter they do not cultivate, even to uniformity, the physical, intellectual, and moral faculties; and lastly and especially, the prevalence of certain determining ideas, more binding than laws, suppress those energies which are the source of every active virtue, and the indispensable condition of any higher and more various culture. With the ancients, moreover, the increase of force served to compensate for their uniformity; but with the moderns uniformity is aggravated by the evil of diminished energy. This difference between the States of antiquity and those of our own times, is in general thoroughly evident. Whilst in these later centuries, the rapid strides of progress, the number and dissemination of artistic inventions, and the enduring grandeur of establishments, especially attract our attention; antiquity captivates us above all by that inherent greatness which is comprised in the life of the individual, and perishes along with him,—the bloom of fancy, the depth of thought, the strength of will, the perfect oneness of the entire being, which alone confer true worth on human nature. Their strong consciousness of this essential worth of human nature, of its powers and their consistent development, was to them the quick impulse to every manifestation of activity; but these seem to us but as abstractions, in which the sense of the individual is lost, or at least in which his inner life is not so much regarded as his ease, his material comfort, his happiness. The ancients sought for happiness in virtue; the moderns have too long been endeavouring to develope the latter from the former;* and even he† who could conceive and portray morality in its purest form, thinks himself bound to supply happiness to his ideal of human nature through the medium of a highly artificial machinery, and this rather as a reward from without, than as a boon obtained by man's own exertions. I need not trace any further the features of this striking difference, but will draw these hints to a conclusion with an illustrative passage from Aristotle's Ethics :—" For that which peculiarly belongs to each by nature, is best and most pleasant to every one; and consequently, to man, the life according to intellect (is most pleasant), if intellect especially constitutes Man. This life therefore is the most happy ‡."

It has been from time to time disputed by publicists,

---

* This difference is never so strikingly evident as when we make the comparison between the ancient and modern philosophers. In place of other illustration, I quote some remarks of Tiedemann on one of the finest passages in Plato's Republic :—" Quanquam autem per se sit justitia grata nobis : tamen si exercitium ejus nullam omnino afferret utilitatem, si justo ea omnia essent patienda, quæ fratres commemorant; injustitia justitiæ foret præferenda; quæ enim ad felicitatem maxime faciunt nostram, sunt absque dubio aliis præponenda. Jam corporis cruciatus, omnium rerum inopia, fames, infamia, quæque alia evenire justo fratres dixerunt, animi illam e justitia manantem voluptatem dubio procul longe superant, essetque adeo injustitia justitiæ antehabenda et in virtutum numero collocanda." (Tiedemann in argumentis dialogorum Platonis. Ad 1. 2, de Republica.)—" Now although justice is pleasing to us in its own nature, still if the practice of it did not confer any advantage whatever, if the just man had to endure all that the brothers relate, injustice would be preferable to justice; for the things which especially contribute to our happiness, are unquestionably to be preferred to others. Now bodily torture, utter indigence, hunger, infamy, and whatever else the brothers observed to befall the just man, far outweigh, doubtless, that spiritual pleasure which flows from justice; and so injustice would have to be preferred to justice, and ranked in the number of virtues."

† Kant, on the *Summum Bonum*, in his Elements of Moral Metaphysics (Riga, 1785), and in the Critique of Practical Reason.

‡ Τὸ γὰρ οἰκεῖον ἑκάστῳ τῇ φύσει κράτιστον καὶ ἥδιστόν ἐστιν ἑκάστῳ· καὶ τῷ ἀνθρώπῳ δὴ ὁ κατὰ τὸν νοῦν βίος, εἴπερ μάλιστα τοῦτο ἄνθρωπος· οὗτος ἄρα καὶ εὐδαιμονέστατος.—Arist. Eth. Nich. bk. x. ch. 7 sub fin.

whether the State should provide for the security only, or for the whole physical and moral well-being of the nation. The vigilant solicitude for the freedom of private life has in general led to the former proposition; while the idea that the State can bestow something more than mere security, and that the injurious limitation of liberty, although a possible, is not an essential, consequence of such a policy, has disposed many to the latter opinion. And this belief has undoubtedly prevailed, not only in political theory, but in actual practice. Ample evidence of this is to be found in most of the systems of political jurisprudence, in the more recent philosophical codes, and in the history of Constitutions generally. The introduction of these principles has given a new form to the study of politics (as is shown for instance by so many recent financial and legislative theories), and has produced many new departments of administration, as boards of trade, finance, and national economy. But, however generally these principles may be accepted, they still appear to me to require a more radical investigation; and this can only proceed from a view of human nature in the abstract, and of the highest ends of human existence.

# CHAPTER II.

## OF THE INDIVIDUAL MAN, AND THE HIGHEST ENDS OF HIS EXISTENCE.

THE true end of Man, or that which is prescribed by the eternal and immutable dictates of reason, and not suggested by vague and transient desires, is the highest and most harmonious development of his powers to a complete and consistent whole.  Freedom is the grand and indispensable condition which the possibility of such a development pre-supposes; but there is besides another essential,—intimately connected with freedom, it is true,—a variety of situations. Even the most free and self-reliant of men is thwarted and hindered in his development by uniformity of position. But as it is evident, on the one hand, that such a diversity is a constant result of freedom, and on the other, that there is a species of oppression which, without imposing restrictions on man himself, gives a peculiar impress of its own to surrounding circumstances; these two conditions, of freedom and variety of situation, may be regarded, in a certain sense, as one and the same.  Still, it may contribute to perspicuity to point out the distinction between them.

Every human being, then, can act with but one force at the same time: or rather, our whole nature disposes us at any given time to some single form of spontaneous activity. It would therefore seem to follow from this, that man is inevitably destined to a partial cultivation, since he only enfeebles his energies by directing them to a multiplicity of objects.  But we see the fallacy of such a conclusion when we reflect, that man has it in his power to avoid this one-sidedness, by striving to unite the separate faculties of his nature, often singly exercised; by bringing into spontaneous co-operation, at each period of his life, the gleams of activity about to expire, and those which the future alone will kindle into living effulgence; and endeavouring to increase and diversify the powers with which he works, by harmoniously combining them, instead of looking for a mere variety of objects for their separate exercise. That which is effected, in the case of the individual, by the union of the past and future with the present, is produced in society by the mutual co-operation of its different single members; for, in all the stages of his existence, each individual can exhibit but one of those perfections only, which represent the possible features of human character. It is through such social union, therefore, as is based on the internal wants and capacities of its members, that each is enabled to participate in the rich collective resources of all the others. The experience of all, even the rudest, nations, furnishes us an example of a union thus formative of individual character, in the union of the sexes. And, although in this case the expression, as well of the difference as of the longing for union, appears more marked and striking, it is still no less active in other kinds of association where there is actually no difference of sex; it is only more difficult to discover in these, and may perhaps be more powerful for that very reason. If we were to follow out this idea, it might perhaps conduct us to a clearer insight into the phenomena of those unions so much in vogue among the ancients, and more especially the Greeks, among whom we find them countenanced even by the legislators themselves: I mean those so frequently, but unworthily, classed under the general appellation of ordinary love, and sometimes, but always erroneously, designated as mere friendship. The efficiency of all such unions as instruments of cultivation, wholly depends on the degree in which the component members can succeed in combining their personal independence with the intimacy of the common bond; for whilst, without this intimacy, one individual cannot sufficiently possess himself, as it were, of the nature of the others, independence is no less essential, in order that the perceived be assimilated into the being of the perceiver. Now, it is clear (to apply these conclusions to the respective conditions for culture,—freedom, and a variety of situations), that, on the one hand, individual energy is essential to the perceived and perceiver, into which social unions may be resolved; and, on the other, a difference between them, neither so great as to prevent the one from comprehending the other, nor so inconsiderable as to exclude admiration for that which the other possesses, and the desire of assimilating it into the perceiver's character.

This individual vigour, then, and manifold diversity, combine themselves in *originality;* and hence, that on which the consummate grandeur of our nature ultimately depends, —that towards which every human being must ceaselessly direct his efforts, and on which especially those who design to influence their fellow men must ever keep their eyes, is the *Individuality of Power and Development.* Just as this individuality springs naturally from the perfect freedom of action, and the greatest diversity in the agents, it tends immediately to produce them in turn. Even inanimate nature, which, proceeding in accordance with unchangeable laws, advances by regular grades of progression, appears more individual to the man who has been developed in his individuality. He transports himself, as it were, into the very centre of nature; and it is true, in the highest sense, that each still perceives the beauty and rich abundance of the outer world, in the exact measure in which he is conscious of their existence in his own soul. How much sweeter and closer must this correspondence become between effect and cause,—this reaction between internal feeling and outward perception,—when man is not only passively open to external sensations and impressions, but is himself also an agent!

If we attempt to confirm these principles by a closer application of them to the nature of the individual man, we find that everything which enters into the latter, reduces itself to the two elements of Form and Substance. The purest form, beneath the most delicate veil, we call Idea; the crudest substance, with the most imperfect form, we call sensuous Perception. Form springs from the union of substance. The richer and more various the substance that is united, the more sublime is the resulting form. A child of the gods is the offspring only of immortal parents: and as the blossom swells and ripens into fruit, and from the tiny germ imbedded in its soft pulp the new stalk shoots forth, laden with newly-clustering buds; so does the Form become in turn the substance of a still more exquisite Form. The intensity of power, moreover, increases in proportion to the greater variety and delicacy of the substance; since the internal cohesion increases with these. The substance seems as if blended in the form, and the form merged in the substance. Or, to speak without metaphor, the richer a man's feelings become in ideas, and his ideas in feelings, the more lofty and transcendent his sublimity; for upon this constant intermingling of form and substance, or of diversity with the individual unity, depends the perfect interfusion of the two natures which co-exist in man, and upon this, his greatness. But the force of the generation depends upon the energy of the generating forces. The consummating point of human existence is the flowering of these forces*. In the vegetable world, the

* *Blüthe, Reife.* Neues deutsches Museum, 1791. Junius 22, 3.

simple and less graceful form of the fruit seems to prefigure
the more perfect bloom and symmetry of the flower which
it precedes, and which it is destined gradually to unfold.
Everything conspires to the beautiful consummation of the
blossom. That which first shoots forth from the little
germ is not nearly so exquisite and fascinating. The full
thick trunk, the broad leaves rapidly detaching themselves
from each other, seem to require some fuller and fairer development; as the eye glances up the ascending stem, it
marks the spiring grades of this development; more tender
leaflets seem longing to unite themselves, and draw closer
and closer together, until the central calyx of the crowning
flower seems to give the sweet satisfaction to this growing
desire*. But destiny has not blessed the tribe of plants in
this the law and process of their growth. The flower fades
and dies, and the germ of the fruit reproduces the stem, as
rude and unfinished as the former, to ascend slowly through
the same stages of development as before. But when, in
man, the blossom fades away, it is only to give place to
another still more exquisitely beautiful; and the charm of
the last and loveliest is only hidden from our view in the
endlessly receding vistas of an inscrutable eternity. Now,
whatever man receives externally, is only as the grain of
seed. It is his own active energy alone that can convert
the germ of the fairest growth, into a full and precious
blessing for himself. It leads to beneficial issues only when
it is full of vital power and essentially individual. The
highest ideal, therefore, of the co-existence of human beings,
seems to me to consist in a union in which each strives to
develope himself from his own inmost nature, and for his own
sake. The requirements of our physical and moral being
would, doubtless, bring men together into communities;
and even as the conflicts of warfare are more honourable

* Goethe, über die Metamorphose der Pflanzen.

than the fights of the arena, and the struggles of exaspe-
rated citizens more glorious than the hired and unsympa-
thizing efforts of mere mercenaries, so would the exerted
powers of such spontaneous agents succeed in eliciting the
highest and noblest energies.

And is it not exactly this which so unspeakably captivates
us in contemplating the life of Greece and Rome, and which
in general captivates any age whatever in the contemplation
of a remoter one? Is it not that these men had harder
struggles to endure with the ruthless force of destiny, and
harder struggles with their fellow men? that greater and
more original energy and individuality constantly encountered each other, and gave rise in the encounter to ever
new and beautiful forms? Every later epoch,—and in
what a rapid course of declension must this now proceed!—
is necessarily inferior in variety to that which it succeeded:
in variety of nature,—the boundless forests have been
cleared, the vast morasses dried up; in variety of human
life, by the ever-increasing intercommunication and union
of all human establishments*. It is in this we find one of
the chief causes which render the idea of the new, the uncommon, the marvellous, so much more rare,—which make
affright or astonishment almost a disgrace,—and not only
render the discovery of fresh and, till now, unknown expedients, far less necessary, but also all sudden, unpremedi-
tated and urgent decisions. For, partly, the pressure of
outward circumstances is less violent, while man is provided
with more ample means for opposing them; partly, this
resistance is no longer possible with the simple forces which
nature bestows on all alike, fit for immediate application;
and, in fine, partly a higher and more extended knowledge
renders inventions less necessary, and the very increase of
learning serves to blunt the edge of discovery. It is, on the

* Rousseau has also noticed this in his 'Emile.'

other hand, undeniable that, whereas physical variety has so vastly declined, it has been succeeded by an infinitely richer and more satisfying intellectual and moral variety, and that our superior refinement can recognize more delicate differences and gradations, and our disciplined and susceptible character, if not so firmly consolidated as that of the ancients, can transfer them into the practical conduct of life,— differences and gradations which might have wholly escaped the notice of the sages of antiquity, or at least would have been discernible by them alone. To the human family at large, the same has happened as to the individual: the ruder features have faded away, the finer only have remained. And in view of this sacrifice of energy from generation to generation, we might regard it as a blessed dispensation if the whole human species were as one man ; or the living force of one age could be transmitted to the succeeding one, along with its books and inventions. But this is far from being the case. It is true that our refinement possesses a peculiar force of its own, perhaps even surpassing the former in strength, just in proportion to the measure of its refinement; but it is a question whether the prior development, through the more robust and vigorous stages, must not always be the antecedent transition. Still, it is certain that the sensuous element in our nature, as it is the earliest germ, is also the most vivid expression of the spiritual.

Whilst this is not the place, however, to enter on the discussion of this point, we are justified in concluding, from the other considerations we have urged, that we must at least preserve, with the most eager solicitude, all the force and individuality we may yet possess, and cherish aught that can tend in any way to promote them.

I therefore deduce, as the natural inference from what has been argued, *that reason cannot desire for man any other condition than that in which each individual not only enjoys the most absolute freedom of developing himself by his own energies, in his perfect individuality, but in which external nature even is left unfashioned by any human agency, but only receives the impress given to it by each individual of himself and his own free will, according to the measure of his wants and instincts, and restricted only by the limits of his powers and his rights.*

From this principle it seems to me, that Reason must never yield aught save what is absolutely required to preserve it. It must therefore be the basis of every political system, and must especially constitute the starting-point of the inquiry which at present claims our attention.

# CHAPTER III.

## ON THE SOLICITUDE OF THE STATE FOR THE POSITIVE WELFARE OF THE CITIZEN.

KEEPING in view the conclusions arrived at in the last chapter, we might embody in a general formula our idea of State agency when restricted to its just limits, and define its objects as all that a government could accomplish for the common weal, without departing from the principle just established; while, from this position, we could proceed to derive the still stricter limitation, that any State interference in private affairs, not directly implying violence done to individual rights, should be absolutely condemned. It will be necessary, however, to examine in succession the different departments of a State's usual or possible activity, before we can circumscribe its sphere more positively, and arrive at a full solution of the question proposed.

A State, then, has one of two ends in view; it designs either to promote happiness, or simply to prevent evil; and in this latter case, the evil which arises from natural causes, or that which springs from man's disregard for his neighbour's rights. If it restricts its solicitude to the second of these objects, it aims merely at security; and I would here oppose this term security to every other possible end of State agency, and comprise these last under the general head of Positive Welfare. Further, the various means adopted by a State, as subservient to its purposes, affect in very different measure the extension of its activity. It may endeavour, for instance, to secure the accomplishment of these immediately, either with the aid of coercion or by the inducements of example and exhortation; or it may combine all these sources of influence in the attempt to shape the citizen's outward life in accordance with its ends, and forestal actions contrary to its intention; or, lastly, it may try to exercise a sway over his thoughts and feelings, so as to bring his *inclinations*, even, into conformity with its wishes. It will be evident, that it is single actions only that come under political supervision in the first of these cases; that this is extended in the second to the general conduct of life; and that, in the last instance we have supposed, it is the very character of the citizen, his views, and modes of thought, which are brought under the influence of State control. The actual working of this restrictive agency, moreover, is clearly least considerable in the first of these cases, more so in the second, and is most effective and apparent in the last; either because, in this, it reaches the most copious sources of action, or that the very possibility of such an influence presupposes a greater multiplicity of institutions. But however seemingly different the departments of political action to which they respectively belong, we shall scarcely find any one institution which is not more or less intimately interwoven, in its objects or its consequences, with several of these. We have but to notice, by way of illustration, the close interdependence that exists between the promotion of welfare and the maintenance of security; and further, to remember that when any influence affecting single actions only, engenders a habit through the force of repetition, it comes ultimately to modify the character itself. Hence, in view of this interdependence of political institutions, it becomes very difficult to discover a systematic division of the whole subject before us, sufficiently correspondent to the course of our present inquiry. But, in any case, it will be most immediately conducive to our design, to examine in the outset whether the State should extend its solicitude to the positive welfare of the nation, or content itself with provisions for its security; and, confining our view of institutions to what is strictly essential either in their objects or consequences, to ascertain next, as regards both of these aims, the nature of the means that may be safely left open to the State for accomplishing them.

I am speaking here, then, of the entire efforts of the State to elevate the positive welfare of the nation; of its solicitude for the population of the country, and the subsistence of its inhabitants, whether manifested directly in such institutions as poor-laws, or indirectly, in the encouragement of agriculture, industry, and commerce; of all regulations relative to finance and currency, imports and exports, etc. (in so far as these have this positive welfare in view); finally, of all measures employed to remedy or prevent natural devastations, and, in short, of every political institution designed to preserve or augment the physical welfare of the nation. For the moral welfare is not in general regarded so much for its own sake, as with reference to its bearing on security, and will therefore be more appropriately introduced in the subsequent course of the inquiry.

Now all such institutions, I maintain, are positively hurtful in their consequences, and wholly irreconcilable with a true system of polity; a system which, although conceivable only from the loftiest points of view, is yet in no way inconsistent with the limits and capacities of human nature.

1. A spirit of governing predominates in every institution of this kind; and however wise and salutary such a spirit may be, it invariably superinduces national uniformity, and a constrained and unnatural manner of action. Instead of men grouping themselves into communities in order to discipline and develope their powers, even though,

to secure these benefits, they should forego a portion of their exclusive possessions and enjoyments; it is only by the actual *sacrifice* of those powers that they can purchase in this case the privileges resulting from association. The very variety arising from the union of numbers of individuals is the highest good which social life can confer, and this variety is undoubtedly merged into uniformity in proportion to the measure of State interference. Under such a system, it is not so much the individual members of a nation living united in the bonds of a civil compact; but isolated subjects living in a relation to the State, or rather to the spirit which prevails in its government,—a relation in which the undue preponderance of the State element tends already to fetter the free play of individual energies. Like causes produce like effects; and hence, in proportion as State co-operation increases in extent and efficiency, a common resemblance diffuses itself, not only through all the agents to which it is applied, but through all the results of their activity. And this is the very design which States have in view. They desire nothing so much as comfort, ease, tranquillity; and these are most readily secured when there is little or no discordancy among that which is individual. But that to which man's energies are ever urging him, and towards which he must ceaselessly direct his efforts, is the very reverse of this inertness and uniformity, —it is variety and activity. It is to these alone we are to look for the free development of character in all its vigorous and multiform diversity of phase and manifestation; and, to appeal to the inner motive of the individual man, there can be no one, surely, so far sunk and degraded, as to prefer, for himself personally, comfort and enjoyment to greatness; and he who draws conclusions for such a preference in the case of others, may justly be suspected of misconceiving the essential nobleness of human nature, and of agreeing to transform his fellow-creatures into mere machines.

2. Further, a second hurtful consequence ascribable to such a policy is, that these *positive* institutions tend to weaken the power and resources of the nation.   For as the substance is annihilated by the form which is externally imposed upon it, so does it gain greater richness and beauty from that which is *internally* superinduced by its own spontaneous action; and in the case under consideration it is the form which annihilates the substance,—that which is of itself non-existent suppressing and destroying that which really is existent.   The grand characteristic of human nature is *organization.*   Whatever is to ripen in its soil and expand into a fair maturity, must first have existed therein as the little germ.   Every manifestation of power presupposes the existence of enthusiasm; and but few things sufficiently cherish enthusiasm as to represent its object as a present or future possession.   Now man never regards that which he *possesses* as so much his own, as that which he *does;* and the labourer who tends a garden is perhaps in a truer sense its owner, than the listless voluptuary who enjoys its fruits.   It may be, such reasoning appears too general to admit of any practical application. Perhaps it seems even as though the extension of so many branches of science, which we owe chiefly to political institutions (for the State only can attempt experiments on a scale sufficiently vast), contributed to raise the power of intellect, and collaterally, our culture and character in general. But the intellectual faculties themselves are not necessarily ennobled by every acquisition to our knowledge; and though it were granted that these means virtually effected such a result, it does not so much apply to the entire nation, as to that particular portion of it which is connected with the government.   The cultivation of the understand-

ing, as of any other of man's faculties, is in general effected by his own activity, his own ingenuity, or his own methods of availing himself of the facilities discovered by others. Now, State measures always imply more or less positive control; and even where they are not chargeable with actual coercion, they accustom men to look for instruction, guidance, and assistance from without, rather than to rely upon their own expedients. The only method of instruction, perhaps, of which the State can avail itself, consists in its declaring the best course to be pursued as though it were the result of its investigations, and in enjoining this in some way on the citizen. But, however it may accomplish this, —whether directly or indirectly by law, or by means of its authority, rewards, and other encouragements attractive to the citizen, or, lastly, by merely recommending its propositions to his attention by arguments,—it will always deviate very far from the best system of instruction. For this unquestionably consists in proposing, as it were, all possible solutions of the problem in question, so that the citizen may select, according to his own judgment, the course which seems to him to be the most appropriate; or, still better, so as to enable him to discover the happiest solution for himself, from a careful representation of all the contingent obstacles. It will be evident, in the case of adult citizens, that the State can only adopt this *negative* system of instruction by extending freedom, which allows all obstacles to arise, while it developes the skill, and multiplies the opportunities necessary to encounter them; but, by following out a really national system of education, it can be brought to operate *positively* on the early training and culture of the young. We will take occasion, hereafter, to enter on a close examination of the objection which might be advanced here in favour of these institutions; viz. that in the execution of such important designs as those to

which we refer, it is of far greater moment that the thing
be *done*, than that the person who performs it should be
thoroughly instructed in his task; that the land be well
tilled, than that the husbandman be just the most skilful
agriculturist.

But to continue: the evil results of a too extended solicitude on the part of the State, are still more strikingly
manifested in the suppression of all active energy, and the
necessary deterioration of the moral character. We scarcely
need to substantiate this position by rigorous deductions.
The man who frequently submits the conduct of his actions
to foreign guidance and control, becomes gradually disposed
to a willing sacrifice of the little spontaneity that remains
to him. He fancies himself released from an anxiety which
he sees transferred to other hands, and seems to himself to
do enough when he looks for their leading, and follows
the course to which it directs him. Thus, his notions of
right and wrong, of praise and blame, become confounded.
The idea of the first inspires him no longer; and the painful consciousness of the last assails him less frequently and
violently, since he can more easily ascribe his shortcomings
to his peculiar position, and leave them to the responsibility
of those who have shaped it for him. If we add to this,
that he may not, possibly, regard the designs of the State
as perfectly pure in their objects or execution—should he
find grounds to suspect that not his own advantage only,
but along with it some other bye-scheme is intended, then,
not only the force and energy, but the purity and excellence
of his moral nature is brought to suffer. He now con-
ceives himself not only irresponsible for the performance of
any duty which the State has not expressly imposed upon
him, but exonerated at the same time from every personal
effort to ameliorate his own condition; nay, even shrinks
from such an effort, as if it were likely to open out new

c

opportunities, of which the State might not be slow to avail itself. And as for the laws actually enjoined, he labours, as much as possible, to escape their operation, considering every such evasion as a positive gain. If now we reflect that, as regards a large portion of the nation, its laws and political institutions have the effect of circumscribing the grounds of morality, it cannot but appear a melancholy spectacle to see at once the most sacred duties, and mere trivial and arbitrary enactments, proclaimed from the same authoritative source, and to witness the infraction of both visited with the same measure of punishment. Further, the injurious influence of such a positive policy is no less evident in its effects on the mutual bearing of the citizens, than in those manifestations of its pernicious working to which we have just referred. In proportion as each individual relies upon the helpful vigilance of the State, he learns to abandon to its responsibility the fate and well-being of his fellow-citizens. But the inevitable tendency of such abandonment is to deaden the living force of sympathy, and to render the natural impulse to mutual assistance inactive : or, at least, the reciprocal interchange of services and benefits will be most likely to flourish in its greatest activity and beauty, where the feeling is liveliest that such assistance is the only thing to rely upon; and experience teaches us that those classes of the community which suffer under oppression, and are, as it were, overlooked by the Government, are always cemented together by the closest ties. But wherever the citizen becomes insensible to the interests of his fellow-citizen, the husband will contract feelings of cold indifference to the wife, and the father of a family towards the members of his household.

If men were left wholly to themselves in their various undertakings, and were cut off from all external resources, save those which their own efforts obtained, they would still, whether through their own fault and inadvertence or not, fall frequently into embarrassment and misfortune. But the happiness for which man is plainly destined, is no other than that which his own energies enable him to secure; and the very nature of such a self-dependent position furnishes him means whereby to discipline his intellect and cultivate his character. Are there no instances of such evils, I ask, where State agency fetters individual spontaneity by a too special interference? There are many, doubtless; and the man whom it has habituated to lean on foreign strength for support, is thus given up in critical emergencies to a fate which is truly far more hopeless and deplorable. For, just as the very act of struggling against misfortune, and encountering it with vigorous efforts, tends to lighten the calamity; so do baffled hopes and delusive expectations aggravate and embitter its severity tenfold. In short, to view their agency in the most favourable light, States like those to which we refer too often resemble the physician, who only retards the death of his patient in nourishing his disease. Before there were physicians, only health and death were known.

3. Everything towards which man directs his attention, whether it is limited to the direct or indirect satisfaction of his merely physical wants, or to the accomplishment of external objects in general, presents itself in a closely interwoven relation with his internal sensations. Sometimes, moreover, there co-exists with this external purpose, some impulse proceeding more immediately from his inner being; and often, even, this last is the sole spring of his activity, the former being only implied in it, necessarily or incidentally. The more unity a man possesses, the more freely do these external manifestations on which he decides emanate from the inner springs of his being, and the more frequent

c 2

and intimate is the cooperation of these two sources of
motive, even when he has not freely selected these external
objects.  A man, therefore, whose character peculiarly interests us, although his life does not lose this charm in any
circumstances or however engaged, only attains the most
matured and graceful consummation of his activity, when
his way of life is in harmonious keeping with his character.

In view of this consideration, it seems as if all peasants
and craftsmen might be elevated into artists; that is, into
men who love their labour for its own sake, improve it by
their own plastic genius and inventive skill, and thereby
cultivate their intellect, ennoble their character, and exalt
and refine their enjoyments.   And so humanity would be
ennobled by the very things which now, though beautiful
in themselves, so often go to degrade it.   The more a man
accustoms himself to dwell in the region of higher thoughts
and sensations, and the more refined and vigorous his moral
and intellectual powers become, the more he longs to confine himself to such external objects only as furnish ampler
scope and material for his internal development; or, at
least, to overcome all adverse conditions in the sphere allotted him, and transform them into more favourable phases.
It is impossible to estimate a man's advance towards the
Good and the Beautiful, when his unremitting endeavours
are directed to this one engrossing object, the development
of his inner life; so that, superior to all other considerations, it may remain the same unfailing source, the ultimate
goal of all his labours, and all that is corporeal and external
may seem but as its instrument and veil.

How strikingly beautiful, to select an illustration, is the
historical picture of the character fostered in a people by
the undisturbed cultivation of the soil!   The labour they
bestow on the tillage of the land, and the bounteous harvest
with which it repays their industry, bind them with sweet

fetters to their fields and firesides.  Their participation in the rich blessings of toil, and the common enjoyment of the ample fruits it earns, entwine each family with bonds of love, from whose gentle influence even the steer, the partner of their fatigue, is not wholly excluded.   The seed which must be sown, the fruit which must be garnered—regularly returning, as they do, their yearly increase—instil a spirit of patience, trust, and frugality.  The fact of their receiving everything immediately from the hand of benignant Nature, —the ever-deepening consciousness that, although the hand of man must first scatter the seed, it is not from human agency that the rich repletion of the harvest is derived,— the constant dependence on favourable and unfavourable skies, awaken presentiments of the existence of beings of a higher order, now instinct with dire foreboding, and now full of the liveliest joy—in the rapid alternations of fear and hope—and lead the soul to prayer and grateful praise.  The visible image of the simplest sublimity, the most perfect order, and the gentlest beneficence, mould their lives into forms of simple grandeur and tenderness, and dispose their hearts to a cheerful submission to order and law.   Always accustomed to produce, never to destroy, agriculture is essentially peaceful, and, while far beyond the reach of wrong and revenge, is yet capable of the most dauntless courage when roused to resist the injustice of unprovoked attack, and repel the invaders of its calm and happy contentment.

But, still, it cannot be doubted that freedom is the indispensable condition, without which even the pursuits most happily congenial to the individual nature, can never succeed in producing such fair and salutary influences. Whatever man is inclined to, without the free exercise of his own choice, or whatever only implies instruction and guidance, does not enter into his very being, but still remains alien to his true nature, and is, indeed, effected by him, not so much with human agency, as with the mere exactness of mechanical routine. The ancients, and more especially the Greeks, were accustomed to regard every occupation as hurtful and degrading which was immediately connected with the exercise of physical power, or the pursuit of external advantages, and not exclusively confined to the development of the inner man. Hence, many of their philosophers who were most eminent for their philanthropy, approved of slavery; thereby adopting a barbarous and unjust expediency, and agreeing to sacrifice one part of mankind in order to secure to the other the highest force and beauty. But reason and experience combine to expose the error which lies at the root of such a fallacy. There is no pursuit whatever, nothing with which a man can concern himself, that may not give to human nature some worthy and determinate form, and furnish fair means for its ennoblement. The manner of its performance is the only thing to be considered; and we may here lay down the general rule, that a man's pursuits re-act beneficially on his culture, so long as these, and the energies allied with them, succeed in filling and satisfying the wants of his soul; while their influence is not only less salutary, but even pernicious, when he directs his attention more exclusively to the results to which they conduce, and regards the occupation itself merely as a necessary means. For it is the property of anything which charms us by its own intrinsic worth, to awaken love and esteem, while that which only as a means holds out hopes of ulterior advantage, merely interests us; and the motives of love and esteem tend as directly to ennoble human nature, as those of interest to lower and degrade it. Now, in the exercise of such a positive solicitude as that we are considering, the State can only contemplate results, and establish rules whose observance will most directly conduce to their accomplishment.

Never does this limited point of view conduct to such pernicious issues as in those cases where moral or intellectual ends are the object of human endeavour; or, at least, where some end is regarded for itself, and apart from the consequences which are only necessarily or incidentally implied in it. This becomes evident, for instance, in all scientific researches and religious opinions, in all kinds of human association, and in that union in particular which is the most natural, and, whether we regard the State or the individual, the most vitally important, namely, Matrimony.

Matrimony, or as it may perhaps be best defined, the union of persons of both sexes, based on the very difference of sex, may be regarded in as many different aspects as the conceptions taken of that difference, and as the inclinations of the heart, and the objects which they present to the reason, assume different forms; and such a union will manifest in every man his whole moral character, and especially the force and peculiarity of his powers of sensation. Whether a man is more disposed to the pursuit of external objects, or to the exercise of the inner faculties of his being; whether reason or feeling is the more active principle in his nature; whether he is led to embrace things eagerly, and quickly abandon them, or engages slowly but continues faithfully; whether he is capable of deeper intimacy, or only loosely attaches himself; whether he preserves, in the closest union, more or less self-dependence; and an infinite number of other considerations modify, in a thousand ways, his relations in married life. Whatever form they assume, however, the effects upon his life and happiness are unmistakable; and upon the success or failure of the attempt to find or form a reality in union with the internal harmony of his nature, depends the loftier consummation or the relaxation of his being. This influence manifests itself most forcibly in those men, so peculiarly interesting in their character and actions, who form their perceptions with the greatest ease and delicacy, and retain them most deeply and lastingly. Generally speaking, the female sex may be more justly reckoned in this class than the male; and it is for this reason that the female character is most intimately dependent on the nature of the family relations in a nation. Wholly exempt as she is from most outward occupations, and almost surrounded with those only which leave the soul undisturbed—stronger in what she can be than in what she can do—more full of expression in her calm and quiet, than in her manifested sensations—more richly endowed with all means of immediate, indefinable expression, a more delicate frame, a more moving eye, a more winning voice—destined rather, in her relations with others, to expect and receive, than to advance and approach—naturally weaker in herself, and yet not on that account, but through loving admiration of strength and greatness in another, clinging more closely— ceaselessly striving in the union to receive in common with the united one, to form the received in herself, and reproduce it moulded into new forms of creation—inspired at the same time with the courage which the solicitude of love and the feeling of strength infuse into the soul—not defying resistance, but not succumbing in endurance—WOMAN is, strictly speaking, nearer to the ideal of human nature than man; and whilst it is true that she more rarely reaches it, it may only be that it is more difficult to ascend by the steep, immediate path, than to approach slowly by the winding one. Now, how much such a being—so delicately susceptible, yet so complete in herself, and with whom therefore nothing is without effect—an effect that communicates itself not to a part only, but to the whole of her nature,—how much woman must be disturbed by external mis-relations, can scarcely be estimated. Hence the infinite results to society which depend on the culture of the female character. If it is not somewhat fanciful to suppose that each human excellence represents and accumulates itself, as it were, in some one species of being, we might believe that the whole treasure of morality and order is collected and enshrined in the female character. As the poet profoundly says,

"Man strives for freedom, woman still for order*."

While the former strives earnestly to remove the external barriers which oppose his development, woman's careful hand prescribes that inner restraint within whose limits alone the fulness of power can refine itself to perfect issues; and she defines the circle with more delicate precision, in that her every sense is more faithful to her simple behests, spares her that laborious subtilizing which so often tends to enmesh and obscure the truth, and enables her to see more clearly through the intricate confusion of human relations, and fathom at once the innermost springs of human being.

If it were not superfluous, History would afford sufficient confirmation of the truth we would establish, and exhibit unmistakably the close and invariable connection that exists between national morality and respect for the female sex. The manifest inference we would derive, however, from these considerations on the institution of Matrimony is this: that the effects which it produces are as various as the characters of the persons concerned, and that, as a union so closely allied with the very nature of the respective individuals, it must be attended with the most hurtful consequences when the State attempts to regulate it by law, or through the force of its institutions to make it repose on anything save simple inclination. When we remember, moreover, that the State can only contemplate the final

* " Nach Freiheit strebt der Mann, das Weib nach Sitte."—Goethe's Torquato Tasso, ii. 1.

results in such regulations—as, for instance, Population, Early Training, etc.—we shall be still more ready to admit the justice of this conclusion. It may reasonably be argued that a solicitude for such objects conducts to the same results as the highest solicitude for the most beautiful development of the inner man. For, after careful observation, it has been found that the uninterrupted union of one man with one woman is most conducive to population; and it is likewise undeniable that no other union springs from true, natural, harmonious love. And further, it may be observed that such love leads to no other or different results than those very relations which law and custom tend to establish, such as the procreation of children, family training, community of living, participation in the common goods, the management of external affairs by the husband, and the care of domestic arrangements by the wife. But the radical error of such a policy appears to be, that the law *commands*, whereas such a relation cannot mould itself according to external arrangements, but depends wholly on inclination; and wherever coercion or guidance comes into collision with inclination, they divert it still further from the proper path. Wherefore it appears to me that the State should not only loosen the bonds in this instance, and leave ampler freedom to the citizen, but, if I may apply the principles above stated (now that I am not speaking of matrimony in general, but of one of the many injurious consequences arising from restrictive State institutions, which are in this one especially noticeable), that it should entirely withdraw its active solicitude from the institution of Matrimony, and both generally and in its particular modifications should rather leave it wholly to the free choice of the individuals, and the various contracts they may enter into with respect to it. I should not be deterred from the adoption of this principle by the fear that all family relations might be disturbed, or their manifestation in general impeded; for although such an apprehension might be justified by considerations of particular circumstances and localities, it could not be fairly entertained in an inquiry into the nature of Men and States in general.  For experience frequently convinces us that just where law has imposed no fetters, morality most surely binds; the idea of external coercion is one entirely foreign to an institution which, like Matrimony, reposes only on inclination and an inward sense of duty; and the results of such coercive institutions do not at all correspond to the designs in which they originate.

4. *The solicitude of a State for the positive welfare of its citizens, must further be hurtful, in that it has to operate upon a promiscuous mass of individualities, and therefore does harm to these by measures which cannot meet individual cases.*

5. *It hinders the development of Individuality*\*. . . .* In the moral life of man, and generally in the practical conduct of his actions (in as far as they are guided by the same rules), he still endeavours to keep before his eyes the highest conception of the most individual development of himself and others, is always inspired with this design, and strictly subordinates all other considerations of interest to this pure and spiritual law that he has recognized. But all the phases of human nature in which it admits of culture, consist together in a wonderful relation and interdependence; and while their mutual coherency is more strikingly manifest (if not really more intimate) in the intellectual than in the physical world, it is infinitely more remarkable in the sphere of morality.  Wherefore it follows that men are not to unite themselves together in order to forego any portion of

---

\* The reader is referred to the "Prefatory Remarks" for the explanation of this hiatus.

their individuality, but only to lessen the exclusiveness of
their isolation; it is not the object of such a union to transform one being into another, but to open out approaches
between the single natures; whatever each himself possesses, he is to compare with that which he receives by
communication with others, and, while introducing modifications in his own being by the comparison, not to allow
its force and peculiarity to be suppressed in the process.
For as truth is never found conflicting with truth in the
domain of intellect, so too in the region of morality there
is no opposition between things really worthy of human
nature; and close and varied unions of individual characters are therefore necessary, in order to destroy what cannot co-exist in proximity, and does not, therefore, essentially conduce to greatness and beauty, while they cherish
and foster that which continues to exist without opposition
or disturbance, and render it fruitful in new and more
exquisite issues.  Wherefore it appears to me that the principle of the true art of social intercourse consists in a
ceaseless endeavour to grasp the innermost individuality of
another, to avail oneself of it, and, penetrated with the
deepest respect for it as the individuality of another, to act
upon it,—a kind of action, in which that same respect will
not allow us other means for this purpose than to manifest
oneself, and to institute a comparison, as it were, between
the two natures, before the eyes of the other.   This art has
been hitherto singularly neglected, and although such neglect might borrow a plea, perhaps, from the circumstance
that social intercourse should be a refreshing recreation,
and not a toilsome duty, and that, unhappily enough, it is
scarcely possible to discover in the common run of men an
interesting phase of individuality, yet still it seems not too
much to suppose that every one will have too deep a respect
for himself to seek for recreation otherwise than in an agree-

able alternation of interesting employments, or still less to look for it in that which would leave precisely his noblest faculties inactive, and too much reverence for human nature, to pronounce any single individual utterly incapable of being turned to good account, or of being in some way modified by the influence of others. He, at least, whose especial business it is to exercise an influence over his fellow-men, must not relinquish such a belief; and hence, inasmuch as the State, in its positive solicitude for the external and physical well-being of the citizen (which are closely interwoven with his inner being), cannot avoid creating hindrances to the development of individuality, we derive another reason why such a solicitude should not be conceded to it, except in the case of the most absolute necessity.

These, then, may constitute the principal hurtful consequences which flow from a positive solicitude of the State for the welfare of the citizen; and although they may be more especially implied in certain of its particular manifestations, they yet appear to me to be generally inseparable from the adoption of such a policy. It was my design hitherto to confine myself to a view of the State's solicitude for physical welfare, and I have so far accorded with this intention as to proceed strictly from this point of view alone, carefully separating everything that referred exclusively to the moral well-being. But I took occasion at the outset to mention that the subject does not admit of any accurate division; and this may serve as my excuse, if much that naturally arises from the foregoing development of the argument, applies to the entire solicitude for positive welfare in general. I have hitherto proceeded on the supposition, however, that the State institutions referred to are already established, and I have therefore still to speak of certain difficulties which present themselves in the very framing of such institutions.

6. It is certain, then, that nothing would be more conducive to the successful issue of our present inquiry, than to weigh the advantages intended by such institutions against the disadvantages necessarily inherent in their consequences, and especially against the limitations of freedom which these consequences imply. But it is always a matter of extreme difficulty to effect such a balancing of results, and perhaps wholly impossible to secure its perfect accuracy and completeness. For every restrictive institution comes into collision with the free and natural development of power, and gives rise to an infinite multiplicity of new relations; and even if we suppose the most equable course of events, and set aside all serious and unlooked-for accidents, the number of these relations which it brings in its train is not to be foreseen. Any one who has an opportunity of occupying himself with the higher departments of State administration, must certainly feel conscious from experience how few political measures have really an immediate and absolute necessity, and how many, on the contrary, have only a relative and indirect importance, and are wholly dependent on foregone measures. Now, in this way a vast increase of means is rendered necessary, and even these very means are drawn away from the attainment of the true end. Not only does such a State require larger sources of revenue, but it needs in addition an increase of artificial regulations for the maintenance of mere political security: the separate parts cohere less intimately together —the supervision of the Government requires far more vigilance and activity. Hence comes the calculation, no less difficult, but unhappily too often neglected, whether the available resources of the State are adequate to provide the means which the maintenance of security demands; and should this calculation reveal a real misproportion, it only suggests the necessity of fresh artificial arrangements,

which, in the end, overstrain the elasticity of the power—an evil from which (though not from this cause only) many of our modern States are suffering.

We must not overlook here one particular manifestation of this generally injurious agency, since it so closely affects human development; and this is, that the very administration of political affairs becomes in time so full of complications, that it requires an incredible number of persons to devote their time to its supervision, in order that it may not fall into utter confusion.   Now, by far the greater portion of these have to deal with the mere symbols and formulas of things; and thus, not only men of first-rate capacity are withdrawn from anything which gives scope or stimulus to the thinking faculties, and men who would be usefully employed in some other way are diverted from their real course of action, but their intellectual powers are brought to suffer from this partly fruitless, partly one-sided employment.   Wholly new sources of gain, moreover, are introduced and established by this necessity of despatching State affairs, and these render the servants of the State more dependent on the governing classes of the community than on the nation in general.   Familiar as they have become to us in experience, we need not pause to describe the numerous evils which flow from such a dependence—what looking to the State for help, what a lack of self-reliance, what false vanity, what inaction even, and want.   The very evils from which these hurtful consequences flow, are immediately produced by them in turn.   When once thus accustomed to the transaction of State affairs, men gradually lose sight of the essential object, and limit their regard to the mere form; they are thus prompted to attempt new ameliorations, perhaps true in intention, but without sufficient adaptation to the required end; and the prejudicial operation of these necessitates new forms, new complications, and often new restrictions, and thereby creates new departments, which require for their efficient supervision a vast increase of functionaries. Hence it arises that in every decennial period the number of the public officials and the extent of registration increase, while the liberty of the subject proportionately declines. In such an administration, moreover, it follows of course that everything depends on the most vigilant supervision and careful management, since there are such increased opportunities of falling short in both; and hence we may not unjustly suppose the Government desirous that everything should pass through as many hands as possible, in order to defeat the risk of errors and embezzlement.

But according to this method of transacting affairs, business becomes in time merely mechanical, while the men who are engaged in it relapse into machines, and all genuine worth and honesty decline in proportion as trust and confidence are withdrawn. Finally, as the occupations we refer to must be vested with high importance, and must in consequence really acquire that importance in men's opinion, the idea of what is momentous or trivial, of what is dignified or contemptible, of what are essential and what are subordinate aims, must soon be wholly reversed. Admitting, in conclusion, that the actual necessity for occupations of this nature compensates, on the other hand, by many beneficial results, for the introduction of these manifold evils, I will not here dwell longer on this part of the subject, but will proceed at once to the ultimate consideration—to which all that has hitherto been educed is but the necessary prelude and preparation,—and endeavour to show how the positive solicitude of a State tends utterly to confound all just and natural points of view.

7. In the kind of policy we are supposing, then, men are neglected for things, and powers for results. A political

community, organized and governed according to this system, resembles rather an accumulated mass of living and lifeless instruments of action and enjoyment, than a multitude of acting and enjoying powers. In disregarding the spontaneity of acting beings, they seem to confine their view to the attainment of happiness and enjoyment alone. But although the calculation would be just, inasmuch as the sensation of him who experiences them is the best index of happiness and enjoyment, it would still be very far below the dignity of human nature. For how could we account for it otherwise, that this very system, which aims at tranquillity, should yet, as if apprehensive of the contrary, willingly resign the highest human enjoyment? Joy is greatest in those moments in which man is sensible of having attained the highest reach of his faculties, and is most deeply conscious of the entirety of his nature. It is doubtless true that at such times also he is nearest the depth of his greatest misery; for the moment of intensity can only be succeeded by a like intensity, and the impulse to joy or despair remains ever in the hands of invincible fate. But when the feeling of the highest in human nature truly deserves the name of happiness, even pain and suffering assume another character. The inmost heart of man is the true seat of happiness or misery, nor does his feeling fluctuate with the billowy tide of circumstance on which he is borne. The system we have condemned only leads us to a fruitless struggle to escape pain. But he who truly knows the nature of enjoyment can endure and resign himself to pain, which, in spite of all, still speeds on the footsteps of the fugitive; thus he learns to rejoice unceasingly in the steady, onward march of destiny; and the prospect of greatness still sweetly allures him, whether growing up before his admiration in the present, or fleeing away from his eyes into the dimly-receding future. Thus he comes to the feeling (so rare except to the enthusiast) that even the moment in which he is most deeply sensible of destruction, may be a moment of the highest ecstasy.

Perhaps I may be charged with having exaggerated the evils here enumerated; but, allowing that they may be materially modified in their operation, according to the degree and method of State interference, I must repeat, with this reservation, that it was my task to follow out the working of that interference to its fullest and furthest consequences. With regard to the whole conduct of the inquiry, I would desire that all considerations of a general nature contained in these pages, be viewed entirely apart from the reality of actual practice. In this reality we do not often find any case fully and purely developed,—we do not see the true working of single elements, separate and by themselves. And it is not to be forgotten, in such a consideration of causes and effects, that when once noxious influences are set in operation, the course of ruin towards which they impel, progresses with rapidly accelerating strides. Just as a greater force united to a greater produces results doubly multiplied in their magnitude and importance; so does a less in conjunction with a less quickly degenerate to infinitesimal issues, which baffle the subtlest penetration to follow them in their rapid grades of declension. Should we even concede, however, that these consequences might be less fatal, the opposite theory would still approve itself the happiest in the truly inestimable blessings that must flow from the application of its principles, if that application should ever be wholly possible. For the ever-restless impulsive force inherent in the very nature of things, incessantly struggles against the operation of every pernicious institution, while it promotes as actively everything of a beneficial tendency; so that we may accept it in the highest sense as true, that the sum of evil produced at any time, even by the

most determined eagerness and activity, can never equal
the fair amount of good that is everywhere and at all times
spontaneously effected.

I could here present an agreeable contrast of a people in
the enjoyment of absolute, unfettered freedom, and of the
richest diversity of individual and external relations; I
could exhibit how, even in such a condition, fairer and loftier and more wonderful forms of diversity and originality
must still be revealed, than even any in that antiquity which
so unspeakably fascinates, despite the harsher features which
must still characterize the individuality of a ruder civilization; a condition in which force would still keep pace with
refinement, and even with the rich resources of revealed
character, and in which, from the endlessly ramified inter-
connection between all nations and quarters of the globe,
the very elements themselves would seem more numerous;
I could then proceed to show what new force would bloom
out and ripen into fruition, when every existing thing was
organizing itself by its own unhindered agency; when even
surrounded, as it would be, by the most exquisite forms, it
transformed these present shapes of beauty into its own internal being with that unhampered spontaneity which is the
cherished growth of freedom : I could point out with what
delicacy and refinement the inner life of man would unfold
its strength and beauty; how it would in time become the
high, ultimate object of his solicitude, and how everything
physical and external would be transfused into the inner
moral and intellectual being, and the bond which connects
the two natures together would gain lasting strength, when
nothing intervened to disturb the reaction of all human
pursuits upon the mind and character : how no single agent
would be sacrificed to the interest of another; but while
each held fast the measure of power bestowed on him, he
would for that very reason be inspired with a still lovelier

eagerness to give it a direction conducive to the benefit of
the others: how, when every one was progressing in his individuality, more varied and exquisite modifications of the
beautiful human character would spring up, and onesidedness would become more rare, as it is the result of feebleness
and insufficiency; and as each, when nothing else would
avail to make the other assimilate himself to him, would be
more effectually constrained to modify his own being by the
still continuing necessity of union with others: how, in
such a people, no single energy or hand would be lost to
the task of ennobling and enhancing human existence: and
lastly, how through this focal concentration of energies, the
views of all would be directed to this last end alone, and
would be turned aside from every other object that was
false or less worthy of humanity. I might then conclude,
by showing how the beneficial consequences of such a constitution, diffused throughout the people of any nation
whatever, would even remove an infinite share of the fright-
fulness of that human misery which is never wholly eradi-
cable, of the destructive devastations of nature, of the fell
ravages of hostile animosity, and of the wanton luxurious-
ness of excessive indulgence in pleasure. But I content
myself with having limned out the more prominent features
of the contrasting picture in a general outline; it is enough
for me to throw out a few suggestive ideas, for riper judg-
ments to sift and examine.

If we come now to the ultimate result of the whole argument we have been endeavouring to develope, the first
principle we eliminate will be, that *the State is to abstain
from all solicitude for the positive welfare of the citizens,
and not to proceed a step further than is necessary for their
mutual security and protection against foreign enemies; for
with no other object should it impose restrictions on freedom.*

The means through which such a solicitude manifests

itself in action, would now naturally present themselves for our consideration; but, as the principles we seek to establish wholly disapprove of the thing itself, it is needless to dwell on these. It may be generally observed however, in connection with this subject, that the means by which freedom is limited with a view to welfare are very various in their character, as laws, exhortations, premiums, which are direct in their operation, and immunities, monopolies, etc. and the power acquired by the sovereign as chief landowner, which are indirect; and that all of them, whether direct or indirect, or however they may differ in kind or degree, are attended with pernicious consequences. Should it be objected to these assertions that it appears somewhat strange to deny to the State a privilege which is accorded to every individual, viz. to propose rewards, to extend loans, to be a land-owner, the objection might be fairly entertained if it were possible for the State to consist of a double personality in practice, as it does in theory. In such a case it would be the same as if a private individual had secured to himself a vast amount of influence. But when we reflect (still keeping theory clear from practice) that the influence of a private person is liable to diminution and decay, from competition, dissipation of fortune, nay even death; and that clearly none of these contingencies can be applied to the State; there still remains the unassailable principle that the latter is not to meddle in anything which does not refer exclusively to security,—a principle whose force of apposition is enhanced in that it has not been supported by arguments derived from the very nature of coercion itself. A private person, moreover, acts from other motives than the State. If an individual citizen proposes premiums, which I will agree to suppose are as efficient inducements as those of the State (although this is never perhaps the case), he does so for some interest of his own. Now, from his continual intercourse with his fellow-citizens, and the equality of his condition with theirs, his interest must be closely connected with their advantage or disadvantage, and hence with the circumstances of their respective positions. The end moreover which he designs to attain is already prepared and anticipated in the present, and therefore produces beneficial results. But the grounds on which the State acts are ideas and principles, which often deceive the correctest calculations; and if the reasons be drawn from considerations of its private capacity, it may be observed that this is too often questionable, where the welfare and security of the citizen are concerned, and further, that the capacity of the citizens is never equal in the same degree. Even granting this double personality, it is then no longer the State which acts; and the very nature of such reasoning forbids its application.

The points of view from which these last considerations are suggested, and from which indeed our whole argument proceeds, have no other object than simply man's power, as such, and his internal development. Such reasoning would be justly chargeable with onesidedness if it wholly disregarded the conditions which must exist in order that that power may operate at all. And while mentioning this, we must not overlook the question that naturally arises in this place, viz. whether those very things from which we would withdraw the operation of State solicitude, could ever flourish without it and of themselves. We might here pass before us in successive review, the different kinds of handicraft, agriculture, industry, commerce, and all those distinct departments we have hitherto considered in common, and could bring in the aid of technical knowledge to exhibit the evils and advantages derivable in each case from unhindered freedom, and the abandonment of men to themselves. But, while the want of such technical insight prevents my entering on such a discussion, I am inclined to believe it no longer essential for arriving at the true merits of the question.   Still, if such an investigation could be radically, and, what is especially important, historically conducted, it would not fail to be useful, in that it would tend still more convincingly to approve these ideas, and ascertain at the same time the possibility of their being put in practice, however materially modified,—for the once existing order of things in any political community would scarcely allow of their unmodified application.   Leaving this inquiry however to the proper hands, I shall content myself here with a few general reflections.   Every occupation, then, of whatever nature, is more efficiently performed if pursued for its own sake alone, rather than for the results to which it leads. So deeply grounded is this in human nature, that what has at first been chosen for its utility, in general becomes ultimately attractive in itself.   Now this arises from nothing else than this, that action is dearer to human nature than mere possession, but action only in so far as it is spontaneous.   It is just the most vigorous and energetic who would prefer inactivity to a course of labour to which they are constrained.   Further, the idea of property gains proportionate strength with the idea of freedom, and it is to the feeling of property that we owe the most vigorous activity.   The accomplishment of any great ultimate purpose supposes unity of plan.   This requires no proof; and it is equally true of measures for the prevention of great calamities, famines, inundations, etc.   But this unity might as easily proceed from national as from merely governmental arrangements.   It is only necessary to extend to the nation and its different parts the freedom of entering into contracts.   Between a national and a governmental institution there is always a vast and important difference. That has only an indirect—this, a direct influence; and hence with the former there is always greater freedom of contracting, dissolving, and modifying unions. It is highly probable that all State unions were originally nothing more than such national associations. And here experience shows us the fatal consequences of combining with provisions for security, the attainment of other ultimate ends. Whoever engages in this design must, for the sake of security alone, possess absolute power. But this power he extends to the execution of the remaining projects; and in proportion to its duration and the remoteness from its origin, the power of an institution increases, and the traces of the primary contract vanish. A national measure, however, only retains its proper force in so far as it adheres faithfully to this original compact and its authority. This reason alone might seem sufficient; but, granting even that the fundamental compact was rigidly observed, and that the State union was, in the strictest sense, a national association, still the will of the individuals could only be ascertained through a system of Representation; and it is impossible for the representative of a plurality to be so true an organ of all the opinions of the represented. Now the point to which the whole argument conducts us, is the necessity of securing the consent of every individual. But this very necessity renders the decision by a majority of voices impossible; and yet no other could be imagined in the case of a State union which, in regard to single objects, extended its activity to the positive welfare of the citizen. Nothing would be left to the non-consenting but to withdraw themselves from the community in order to escape its jurisdiction, and prevent the further application of a majority of suffrages to their individual cases. And yet this is almost impossible when we reflect that to withdraw from the social body is just tantamount to separating oneself from the State. We would observe, further, that it is better to enter into separate unions in single associations, than to contract them generally for undetermined future cases; and lastly, that to form associations of free men in a nation is attended with peculiar difficulty. For although this last consideration may seem prejudicial to the attainment of ultimate purposes, it is still certain that every larger association is in general less beneficial; and it should not be forgotten that whatever is produced with difficulty gains from the very fact a more lasting vigour by the implied consolidation of forces long tested and exercised. The more a man acts for himself, the more does he develope himself. In large associations he is too prone to become an instrument merely. A frequent effect of these unions moreover is to allow the symbol to be substituted for the thing, and this always impedes true development. The dead hieroglyphic does not inspire like living nature. In place of other examples I need only instance the case of poor-laws. Does anything tend so effectually to deaden and destroy all true commiseration,—all hopeful yet unobtrusive entreaty,—all loving trustfulness of man in man? Do we not all fitly despise the beggar who rather resigns himself to be fed and nursed in an almshouse than, after sore struggling with want, to find, not a mere hand flinging him a pittance, but a tenderly sympathizing heart? I am willing to admit, in conclusion, that without the mighty masses as it were, with which we have been working in these last centuries, human progress might not have advanced with strides so rapid,—and yet perhaps not rapid alone. The fruit had been longer in expanding and maturing, but still it would really have ripened, and that with a far richer and more precious blessing. Granting this, it is needless to dwell longer on this objection. But two others remain to be tested as we proceed, viz: Whether the maintenance of security even would be possible, with those limitations of the State's activity we have here prescribed? and se-

D

condly, Whether the necessary provision of means for the manifestation of its activity, even when thus limited, does not come to necessitate a more manifold encroachment of the wheels of the State machine, into the relations of the individual citizen ?

# CHAPTER IV.

### OF THE SOLICITUDE OF THE STATE FOR THE NEGATIVE WELFARE OF THE CITIZEN—FOR HIS SECURITY.

To counteract the evil which arises from the tendency man has to transgress his own appropriate limits,* and the discord occasioned by such unjust encroachment on the rights of others, constitutes the essential ground and object of State-union. If it were the same with these subversive manifestations to which we allude, as with the physical violence of nature, or with the working of that moral evil which disturbs the natural order of things through excessive enjoyment or privation, or through other actions inconsistent with that order—then would such unions no longer be necessary. The former, or physical, evil would be encountered by the unaided efforts of human courage, skill, and forethought: the latter, or moral, by the wisdom which is matured in experience ; and with either, in any case, the removal of an evil would be the termination of a struggle. Under such a supposition, therefore, any ultimate, absolute authority, such as properly constitutes the idea of the State, would be wholly unneeded. But, as it is, human variance and discord are utterly different in their nature from these, and positively necessitate at all times the exist-

* What I am here obliged to convey by a circumlocution, the Greeks expressed in the single word, πλεονεξία, for which, however, I do not find an exact equivalent in any other language. We could say, perhaps, in German : 'Begierde nach mehr,' 'a desire for more;' yet still this would not include the notion of *unrightfulness*, which is conveyed in the Greek expression,— at least, if not in the literal meaning of the word, in the constant use of it in their writings. The word 'Uebervortheilung,' 'taking more than one's share,' although still not so full in significance, may approach somewhat nearer to the idea.

D 2

ence of some supreme power like that to which we refer. For in this discordancy one conflict springs immediately from another. Wrong begets revenge; and revenge is but a new wrong. And hence it becomes necessary to look for some species of revenge which does not admit of any other retaliation—that is the punishment inflicted by the State, or for a settlement of the controversy which obliges the the parties to rest satisfied, viz. the decision of the judge. There is nothing, moreover, which necessitates such stringent coercion and such unconditional obedience as man's spirit of enterprise against his fellow-men, whether we regard the expulsion of foreign enemies, or the preservation of security within the State itself. Now, without security, it is impossible for man either to develope his powers, or to enjoy the fruits of his exertion; for, without security, there can be no freedom. But it will be seen at once that this is a condition which man is wholly unable to realize by his own individual efforts; the reasons we have just hinted at serve to show this, and we are confirmed in the conviction by experience; for although we observe that our States are in a far more favourable position than we can conceive that of man in a state of nature to be (closely knit together, as they are, by innumerable treaties and bonds of alliance, and by mutual fear, which so constantly prevents the actual outbreaks of violence)—we must allow, notwithstanding, that they do not possess that freedom which under the most ordinary constitution the very meanest subject enjoys. Whilst, therefore, I have hitherto found reasons for withdrawing the exercise of State solicitude from many important objects, because the nation can accomplish them as effectually and without incurring the evils which flow from State interference, I must for similar reasons direct it to Security as to the only thing* which the individual cannot

* La sûreté et la liberté personnelle sont les seules choses qu'un être isolé ne puisse s'assurer par lui-même.—Mirabeau sur l'Educat. publique, p. 119

obtain for himself and by his own unaided efforts. I would therefore lay down as the first positive principle—a principle to be more carefully defined and limited in the subsequent course of inquiry—that the maintenance of security, as well with regard to the attacks of foreign enemies as to the danger of internal discord, constitutes the true end of the State, and must especially occupy its activity.

Hitherto I have attempted only to define this true end of the State in a negative way, by showing that the latter should not, at least, extend the sphere of its solicitude any further.

If we refer to the pages of history we only find additional confirmation of the position we would establish, in the fact that the kings in all earlier nations were in reality nothing more than leaders in war, and judges in times of peace. I says, kings. For (if I may be pardoned this digression), in those very periods in which men most fondly cherish the feeling of freedom—possessing, as they do, but little property, and only knowing and prizing personal force, and placing the highest enjoyment in its exercise—in those very periods, however strange it may seem, history shows us nothing but kings and monarchies. We observe this in all the Asiatic political unions, in those of the earliest ages of Greece, of Italy, and of those tribes who loved freedom more devotedly than all—the German.* If we examine into the reasons for this seeming contradiction, we are struck with the truth, that the very choice of a monarchy is a proof that those who select that form of government are in the enjoyment of the highest freedom. The idea of a chief ruler arises only, as was before observed, from the deep-felt

* "Reges (nam in terris nomen imperii id primum fuit)," etc.—Sallust in Catilina, c. 2. (Kings—for that was the first title of earthly authority, etc.) Κατ' ἀρχὰς ἅπασα πόλις Ἑλλὰς ἐβασιλεύετο.—Dion. Halicarn. Antiquit. Rom. lib. 5. (All the Grecian States were at first governed by kings, etc.)

necessity for some military leader and umpire of disputes. Now to have one general or umpire is unquestionably the happiest provision for such a necessity. The apprehension that the one person so selected may ultimately become a master is unknown to the man who is truly free; he does not even dream of such a possibility; to no one does he attribute the power of subjugating his liberty, and to no one that is himself free the wish to lord it over others—for he who is utterly insensible to the sublime beauty of liberty and thirsts only for dominion, is in reality in love with slavery, so long as he does not contemplate the likelihood of being himself a slave; and thus it is, that as the science of morals originated in crime, and theology in heresy, so politics sprang into existence with servitude.

And yet, although we find their prototypes in antiquity, it is certain that our monarchs have not the honeyed and persuasive speech which characterized the kings of Homer and Hesiod.*

* Ὅντινα τιμήσουσι Διὸς κοῦραι μεγάλοιο,
Γεινόμενόν τ᾽ ἐσίδωσι διοτρεφέων βασιλήων,
Τῷ μὲν ἐπὶ γλώσσῃ γλυκερὴν χείουσιν ἔερσην,
Τοῦ δ᾽ ἔπε᾽ ἐκ στόματος ῥεῖ μείλιχα.

Τούνεκα γὰρ βασιλῆες ἐχέφρονες, οὕνεκα λαοῖς
Βλαπτόμενοις ἀγορῆφι μετάτροπα ἔργα τελεῦσι
Ῥηϊδίως, μαλακοῖσι παραιφάμενοι ἐπέεσσιν.

Hesiod. Theog. 81. sqq. 88 sqq.

"Whomsoever of the race of kings,—
The foster-sons of Jove,—Jove's daughters will
To honour, on whose infant head, when first
Usher'd to light, they placid gaze from high,
Upon his tongue they shed a balmy dew;
And words, as honey sweet, drop from his lips."

"Lo! in this are kings discreet;
That, in their judgment-hall, they from th' oppress'd
Turn back the tide of ills, retrieving wrongs
With mild accost of soothing eloquence."

C. A. Elton's translation, v. 112. sqq. 122 sqq.

# CHAPTER V.

## ON THE SOLICITUDE OF THE STATE FOR SECURITY AGAINST FOREIGN ENEMIES.

IF it were not conducive to the clearness of our principal idea to apply it successively to single objects, it would not be essential to the present inquiry, to make any reference to the subject of security against foreign enemies. But this brief digression is the less to be regretted, and indeed may not be without illustrative importance, so long as I confine my attention to the influence of war on national character, and regard its institutions from the same point of view that has suggested the master-principle of the whole investigation.

Now, when thus regarded, war seems to be one of the most favourable manifestations for the culture of human nature; and I confess, it is not without regret that I see it disappearing more and more from the scene. However fearful in some aspects, it is still the extremity through which all that active daring—all that endurance and fortitude are steeled and tested, which afterwards work themselves out into such various and beautiful results in the ordinary conduct of life, and which alone impart to its whole form and character that elastic strength and rich diversity, without which facility is feebleness, and unity, inanity.

It may, perhaps, be argued that there are many other means of securing this invigorating discipline in the school of trial and danger—that there are a thousand forms of employment full of mere physical peril, and innumerable crises of moral conflict which assail the firm, unfaltering statesman in the silence of the cabinet, and the free and fearless thinker in his solitary cell. But I cannot divest myself of the belief, that as everything spiritual is but the more exquisite bloom and development of the corporeal, so too, in war, the noblest forms of action and daring are crowned with the fairest moral issues. It is true we still possess, in the eventful past, the strong stem, as it were, from which these active virtues could continue to shoot and bud forth in the present. But the memory of the past is ever dimly receding from our eyes in the distances of oblivion; and while the number of those who fondly cherish its teaching is always diminishing in a nation, its influence even on them tends also gradually to decline. We seldom acknowledge, moreover, in other pursuits, however difficult or perilous, that inherent idea of greatness and glory so inseparably associated with warlike achievement—an idea, based as it is on the conception of superior power, which is far from being chimerical or imaginary.

As for the elements, we do not labour so much to oppose and subdue their antagonism, as to escape their effects and outlast their fury :—

"With the resistless might of gods
Men may not measure strength;"*

—deliverance is not victory; the boon which fate beneficently offers, and of which human courage and susceptibility only avail themselves, is not the fruit or the earnest of superior power. In war, moreover, every one is inspired with the feeling of rights to be defended and wrongs to be avenged; and while man, in a state of nature, esteems it a far higher object to redeem his honour than to accumulate the means

* " Mit Göttern
Soll sich nicht messen
Irgend ein Mensch."
Goethe, in dem Gedicht : Grenzen der Menschheit, ii. p. 69,
Ausg. v. 1840.

of subsistence, it is a choice which even the most civilized would not feel disposed to deny to him.

It will not be supposed for a moment that the death of a fallen warrior has something in it more beautiful to my eyes than the death of the fearless Pliny, or, to instance devotion somewhat too little honoured, the death of Robert and Pilatre du Rozier. But such instances are rare; and it may be fairly questioned whether they would ever, even, occur without the inspiring memory of those former examples. Neither have I selected the most favourable position in the case of war, nor regarded the finer manifestations of its high-souled enthusiasm. Let me recall the Spartans at Thermopylæ, and ask what influence such an illustrious example of heroism in its sons is likely to exercise on the general character of a nation. I do not deny that such a spirit of daring devotedness and self-sacrifice can find room for manifestation in any form or position in life, nor that it actually does thus exhibit itself; but can we blame him, if, as a sentient being, man is most fondly captivated with its most vivid and visible embodiment, or refuse to believe that such a conspicuous expression of courageous virtue exercises the most living and lasting influence on the national spirit and character? And as to the bracing discipline of ordinary life I would observe that, with all that I have heard of evils more terrible than death, I never yet knew any, save the enthusiast, who, while in the full fruition of all the joys of existence, could really afford to despise it. Least of all would we look for such a spirit in antiquity, where as yet the thing itself was superior to the name, and the reality of the present more highly prized than the shadowy uncertainty of the future. My view of the warrior, then, does not apply to such as were trained up and devoted to warlike pursuits in Plato's Republic,* but to men who take life and death,

* These were to be trained to regard death not as something terrible and

like other things, for what they really are, and who, having
the highest in view, can dare to set the highest at stake.
Lastly, it is to be observed that all those situations in
which contrasting extremes are most closely and variously
intermingled, are the deepest and richest in interest, and
conduce most remarkably to human development; but of
what is this so true and so striking a characteristic as of
war—where inclination and duty, and the duty of the man
and that of the citizen, seem ever in irreconcilable conflict,
and where, nevertheless, all these intricate antagonisms find
their clearest and fullest solution, as soon as the spirit of
just defence has put weapons into our hands?

To regard war in this light, in which alone it can be considered as either beneficial or necessary, seems to indicate,
in my opinion, the nature of the policy to be observed by
the State with respect to it.   In order to cherish and promote the nobler spirit which it engenders, and to diffuse it
throughout the whole body of the nation, it will be evident
that freedom is the prime condition.   Now this already argues against the maintenance of standing armies; and we
would observe further, that these and other modern methods and appurtenances of warfare in general, are very far
removed from the ideal we can conceive as most highly conducive to human culture.   If the warrior in general becomes
degraded to a machine as soon as he surrenders his freedom,
this degradation must be still more complete and deplorable
in our methods of conducting war, in which so much less
than formerly depends upon the valour, strength, and skill
of the individual.   How fatal must the uniformity consequent on such a sacrifice become, when, in time of peace, a

to be solicitously avoided, but to be met with indifference and even disdain.
The poets were forbidden to represent Hades as dreadful, but the contrary;
and illustrious men were not to set an enervating example, by giving way to
grief under misfortune.   Vid. Republ. iii. init.—TR.

considerable portion of the nation is condemned to this machine-like existence—not for a few years only, but often
throughout life—merely in the *prospect* of a possible war !
Perhaps it is in nothing so strikingly manifest as in the institutions to which we now refer, that with the progressive
development of the theory of human enterprises, their utility declines as regards the immediate agents concerned. It
cannot be questioned that the art of war has made incredible
strides in advance in modern times, but it is equally unquestionable that the nobler characteristics of the warrior have
proportionately disappeared, and that it is only in antiquity
that we find them flourishing in graceful and consummate
beauty ; or, at least, if this seems exaggerated, that the
warlike spirit appears now to bring little but injurious
consequences in its train for the nations which entertain it,
while in the ancient world we see it so commonly productive
of beneficial results. Our standing armies carry war, so to
speak, into the very bosom of peace. Now, a warlike spirit
is only honourable in union with the fairest virtues which
bloom out from peace, and military discipline, only when
allied with the highest feeling of freedom ; if these are
severed,—and it is needless to show how such a disunion
is promoted by the existence of marshalled armies in the
midst of peace,—the former rapidly degenerates into wild
and lawless ferocity, and the latter into the abject submission of slavery.

Still, although I would condemn the maintenance of
standing armies, it may be well to observe that I only introduce the subject in this place, in so far as it accords with
the immediate scope I have in view. I am far from overlooking their great and undoubted usefulness, which checks
and counterbalances the headlong tendency to ruin, towards
which their faults and disadvantages would inevitably hurry
them like everything else on earth. They are a significant

portion of the whole—the vast web, which has been woven, not by any plans of vain human reason, but by the sure hand of destiny; and the picture that would represent us by the side of our ancestors, fully and fairly delineated in all the complex phases and workings of our modern life, would have to show how mightily they operate on every other characteristic of our age, and how they share with them the praise and blame of all the good or bad that distinguishes it.

I must moreover have been very unfortunate in the exposition of my views, if I am supposed to infer that the State should, from time to time, seek causes for producing war. It may extend the various possibility of freedom to its people, and a neighbouring nation may enjoy a like degree of freedom, which is the only soil where war and every other healthful manifestation of human power arises naturally to meet the necessity and occasion. Men, in every age, are men; nor do they lose their original passions. War will arise of itself; and if, under these circumstances, it should not so arise, it is then at least certain that peace has not been gained by compulsion, nor produced by artificial paralysis; and such a spontaneous tranquillity will be so much the more blessed gift to the nations, as the peaceful ploughman is a more grateful image in our eyes than the blood-stained warrior. And if we conceive of a progressive civilization of the whole human race, it is indeed certain that the later ages will become gradually more peaceful; but in such a development peace will spring from the internal capacities of the beings themselves, and it is the very character of men—free men, that will be imbued with its pure and benevolent spirit. Even now—a single year of European history proves it—we enjoy the fruits of peace, but not a spirit of peacefulness. Human forces, which are ever striving towards an activity that is infinite, either merge in union when they encounter each other, or clash in direct collision.

The form which the conflict of these forces may assume,— whether that of war, or competition, or unknown modifications yet to be revealed,—depends chiefly on the measure of their refinement.

If I may now venture to derive an inference from these reflections accordant with my ultimate design, I would lay down the principle—*that the State should in no way attempt to encourage war, but neither should it forcibly interfere to prevent it, when demanded by necessitous occasion ; that it should allow perfect freedom to the diffusion of warlike impulses through the spirit and character of the nation, while it especially refrains from all positive institutions calculated to foster a national military development ; or, where these last are absolutely necessary—as, for instance, in the training of the citizens to the use of arms—that it should give them a direction likely to induce, not only the skill, daring, and subordination of the mere soldier, but animate those under its discipline with the spirit of true warriors, or rather of noble-minded citizens, ready at all times to fight in the defence of their country.*

# CHAPTER VI.

ON THE SOLICITUDE OF THE STATE FOR THE MUTUAL
SECURITY OF THE CITIZENS.—MEANS FOR ATTAINING
THIS END.—INSTITUTIONS FOR REFORMING THE MIND
AND CHARACTER OF THE CITIZEN.—NATIONAL EDUCA-
TION.

HAVING seen in a preceding chapter that it is not only a
justifiable but necessary end of Government to provide for
the mutual security of the citizens, it here becomes our duty
to enter on a more profound and explicit investigation into
the nature of such a solicitude, and the means through
which it acts. For it does not seem enough merely to
commit the care for security to the political power as a
general and unconditional duty, but it further becomes us
to define the especial limits of its activity in this respect;
or, at least, should this general definition be difficult or
wholly impossible, to exhibit the reasons for that impossibility, and discover the characteristics by which these limits
may, in given cases, be recognized.

Even a very limited range of observation is sufficient to
convince us that this care for preservation may either restrict its efforts to a very narrow sphere, or launch into
bolder measures, and embrace wide and indefinite means of
influence to reach its design. Confined sometimes to the
reparation of irregularities actually committed and the infliction of appropriate punishment, it may embrace, at others,
precautions for preventing their occurrence, or even suggest the policy of moulding the mind and character of the
citizen after the fashion most suitable to its preconceived
scheme of social order. This very extension even of the

governmental plans, admits, so to speak, of different degrees. The violation of personal rights, for example, and any encroachment on the immediate rights of the State, may be carefully investigated and duly reproved, or—by regarding the citizen as accountable to the State for the application of his powers, and therefore as one who robs it, as it were, of its rightful property when he does aught calculated to enfeeble them or disturb their harmonious action— a watchful surveillance may be exercised over those actions even which affect none but the agent himself. I have therefore found it expedient at present to comprise under one head all these varied manifestations of political solicitude, and must therefore be understood to speak of all State-institutions collectively which are dictated by the general design of promoting public security. Meanwhile, it is only necessary to add, that although the very nature of the subject precludes the possibility of any just and accurate division, all those institutions which refer to the moral welfare of the citizen will naturally present themselves in the order of this inquiry; for if they do not, in all cases, aim at security and tranquillity exclusively, these are in general the prominent objects of such institutions. In my manner of discussing the merits and demerits of these, I shall therefore adhere to the system I have hitherto adopted. It will be seen, from the preceding chapters, that I have set out with supposing the utmost extension of State agency conceivable, and then endeavoured, step by step, to ascertain the different provinces from which it should properly be withdrawn, until at length the concern for security is all that has remained to its appropriation. And now it becomes us to adopt, with regard to this general object of security, the same method of procedure; I will therefore begin by supposing the widest acceptation in which the efficient discharge of such a trust can be viewed, in order to arrive, by successive limitations, at those fundamental principles which enable us to determine its true extent. Should such a systematic investigation be regarded as somewhat lengthy and tedious, I am ready to admit that a dogmatic exposition would require a method of treatment exactly the reverse. But, by confining ourselves strictly to inquiry, we can at least be sure of having fully and honestly grappled with the essential subject, and of having omitted nothing of real importance, while unfolding its principles in their natural and consecutive order.

It has, of late, been usual to insist on the expediency and propriety of preventing illegal actions, and of calling in the aid of moral means to accomplish such a purpose; but I will not disguise that, when I hear such exhortations, I am satisfied to think such encroachments on freedom are becoming more rare among us, and in almost all modern constitutions daily less possible.

It is not uncommon to appeal to the history of Greece and Rome in support of such a policy; but a clearer insight into the nature of the constitutions of those ancient nations would at once betray the inconclusiveness of such comparisons. Those States were essentially republics; and such kindred institutions as we find in them were pillars of the free constitution, and were regarded by the citizens with an enthusiasm which rendered their hurtful restrictions on private freedom less deeply felt, and their energetic character less pernicious. They enjoyed, moreover, a much wider range of freedom than is usual among modern States, and anything that was sacrificed was only given up to another form of activity, viz. participation in the affairs of government. Now, in our States, which are in general monarchical, all this is necessarily changed; and whatever moral means the ancients might employ, as national education, religion, moral laws, would under present systems be less fruitful of good results, and productive of far greater injury. We ought not to forget, moreover, in our admiration of antiquity, that what we are so apt to consider the results of wisdom in the ancient legislators, was mostly nothing more than the effect of popular custom, which, only when decaying, required the authority and support of legal sanction. The remarkable correspondency that exists between the laws of Lycurgus and the manners and habits of most uncultivated nations, has already been clearly and forcibly illustrated by Ferguson;* and when we are led to trace the national growth in culture and refinement, we only discern the faint shadow of such early popular institutions. Lastly, I would observe, that men have now arrived at a far higher pitch of civilization, beyond which it seems they cannot aspire to still loftier heights save through the development of individuals; and hence it is to be inferred that all institutions which act in any way to obstruct or thwart this development, and compress men together into vast uniform masses, are now far more hurtful than in earlier ages of the world.

When we regard the working of those moral means which admit of more large and indefinite application, it seems to follow, even from these few and general reflections, that national education—or that which is organized or enforced by the State—is at least in many respects very questionable. The grand, leading principle, towards which every argument hitherto unfolded in these pages directly converges, is the absolute and essential importance of human development in its richest diversity; but national education, since at least it presupposes the selection and appointment of some one instructor, must always promote a definite form of development, however careful to avoid such an error. And hence

* An Essay on the History of Civil Society: Of Rude Nations prior to the Establishment of Property.

it is attended with all those disadvantages which we before observed to flow from such a positive policy; and it only remains to be added, that every restriction becomes more directly fatal, when it operates on the moral part of our nature,—that if there is one thing more than another which absolutely requires free activity on the part of the individual, it is precisely education, whose object it is to develope the individual. It cannot be denied that the happiest results, both as regards the State and the individual, flow from this relation between them,—that the citizen becomes spontaneously active in the State itself, in the form assigned him by his peculiar lot and circumstances, and that by the very contrast or antagonism between the position pointed out to him by the State, and that which he has spontaneously chosen, he is not only himself modified, but the State constitution also is subject to a reciprocal influence; and although the extent and operation of such influences are not of course immediately evident, they are still distinctly traceable in the history of all States, when we keep in view the modifications to which they are subject from the difference of national character. Now this salutary interaction always diminishes in proportion to the efforts made to fashion the citizen's character beforehand, and to train him up from childhood with the express view of becoming a citizen. The happiest result must follow, it is true, when the relations of man and citizen coincide as far as possible; but this coincidence is only to be realized when those of the citizen pre-suppose so few distinct peculiarities that the man may preserve his natural form without any sacrifice; and it is to the expediency of securing this perfect harmony between the requirements of man and citizen that all the ideas I have in view in this inquiry directly converge. For, although the immediately hurtful consequences of such a misrelation as that to which we have referred would be re-

moved when the citizens of a State were expressly trained
up with a view to their political character, still the very
object would be sacrificed which the association of human
beings in a community was designed to secure. Whence I
conclude, that the freest development of human nature, directed as little as possible to ulterior civil relations, should
always be regarded as paramount in importance with respect
to the culture of man in society. He who has been thus
freely developed should then attach himself to the State;
and the State should test and compare itself, as it were, in
him. It is only with such a contrast and conflict of relations, that I could confidently anticipate a real improvement
of the national constitution, and banish all apprehension
with regard to the injurious influence of the civil institutions
on human nature. For even although these were very imperfect, we could imagine how the force of human energies,
struggling against the opposing barriers, and asserting, in
spite of them, its own inherent greatness, would ultimately
prove superior in the conflict. Still, such a result could
only be expected when those energies had been allowed to
unfold themselves in all their natural freedom. For how
extraordinary must those efforts be which were adequate to
maintain and exalt those energies, when even from the period of youth they were bound down and enfeebled by such
oppressive fetters ! Now all systems of national education,
inasmuch as they afford room for the manifestation of a
governmental spirit, tend to impose a definite form on civic
development, and therefore to repress those vital energies
of the nation.

When such a prevailing form of development is definite
in itself, and still beautiful, although one-sided, as we find
it to be in the ancient constitutions and even yet observe it
perhaps in many a republic, there is not only more facility
in its actual working, but it is attended with far less hurt-

ful consequences. But in our monarchical constitutions, happily enough for human development, such a definite form as that which we describe does not at all exist. It clearly belongs to their advantages, however numerous may be the concomitant evils, that inasmuch as the State union is strictly regarded as the means requisite for the desired end, individual power is not necessarily sacrificed to its accomplishment, as is the case with republics. So long as the citizen conducts himself in conformity with the laws, and maintains himself and those dependent on him in comfort, without doing anything calculated to prejudice the interests of the State, the latter does not trouble itself about the particular manner of his existence. Here therefore national education,—which, as such, still keeps in view, however imperceptibly, the culture of the citizen in his capacity of subject, and not, as is the case in private education, the development of the individual man,—would not be directed to the encouragement of any particular virtue or disposition; it would, on the contrary, be designed to realize a balance of all opposing impulses, since nothing tends so much as this to produce and maintain tranquillity, which is precisely the object most ardently desired by States so constituted. But such an artificial equilibrium, as I have before taken occasion to observe, leads at once to utter torpidity and stagnation, or a depression and deficiency of energy; while, on the other hand, the greater regard for single objects which is peculiarly characteristic of private education, operates to produce that equipoise more surely and effectually, by a life of different relations and combinations, and that without any attendant sacrifice of energy.

But even though we were to deny to national education all positive furtherance of particular systems of culture— if we were to represent it as an essential duty that it should simply encourage the spontaneous development of faculties, this would still prove impracticable, since whatever is pervaded by a unity of organization, invariably begets a corresponding uniformity in the actual result, and thus, even when based on such liberal principles, the utility of national education is still inconceivable. If it is only designed to prevent the possibility of children remaining uninstructed, it is much more expedient and less hurtful to appoint guardians where parents are remiss, and extend assistance where they are in indigent circumstances. Further, it is not to be forgotten, that national education fails in accomplishing the object proposed by it, viz. the reformation of morals according to the model which the State considers most conducive to its designs. However great the influence of education may be, and however it may extend to the whole course of a man's actions, still, the circumstances which surround him throughout his whole life are yet far more important. And hence, if all these do not harmonize with its influences, education cannot succeed in effecting its object.

In fine, if education is only to develope a man's faculties, without regard to any definite civil forms to be collaterally imparted to his nature, there is no need of the State's interference. Among men who are really free, every form of industry becomes more rapidly improved,—all the arts flourish more gracefully,—all sciences become more largely enriched and expanded. In such a community, too, domestic bonds become closer and sweeter; the parents are more eagerly devoted to the care of their children, and, in a higher state of welfare, are better able to follow out their desires with regard to them. Among such men emulation naturally arises; and tutors better befit themselves, when their fortunes depend upon their own efforts, than when their chances of promotion rest on what they are led to expect from the State. There would, therefore, be no want of careful family training, nor of those common educational establishments which are so useful and indispensable.* But if national education is to impose some definite form on human nature, it is perfectly certain that there is actually nothing done towards preventing transgressions of law, or establishing and maintaining security. For virtue and vice do not depend on any particular form of being, nor are necessarily connected with any particular aspect of character; in regard to these, much more depends on the harmony or discordancy of all the different features of a man's character—on the proportion that exists between power and the sum of inclinations, etc. Every distinct development of character is capable of its peculiar excess, and to this it constantly tends to degenerate. If then an entire nation has adhered to some certain variety of development, it comes in time to lose all power of resisting the preponderant bias to this one peculiarity, and along with it all power of regaining its equilibrium. Perhaps it is in this that we discover the reason of such frequent changes in the constitution of ancient States. Every fresh constitution exercised an undue influence on the national character, and this, definitely developed, degenerated in turn and necessitated a new one.

Lastly, even if we admit that national education may succeed in the accomplishment of all that it proposes, it effects too much. For in order to maintain the security it contemplates, the reformation of the national morals themselves is not at all necessary. But as my reasons for this position refer to the whole solicitude for morality on the part of the State, I reserve them for the after part

* " Dans une société bien ordonnée, au contraire, tout invite les hommes à cultiver leurs moyens naturels : sans qu'on s'en mêle, l'éducation sera bonne; elle sera même d'autant meilleure, qu'on aura plus laissé à l'industrie des maîtres et à l'émulation des élèves."—Mirabeau, s. l'Educ. Publ. p. 12.

of this inquiry, and proceed meanwhile to consider some single means which are often suggested by that solicitude. I have only to conclude from what has been argued here, that national education seems to me to lie wholly beyond the limits within which political agency should properly be confined.*

* "Ainsi c'est peut-être un problème de savoir, si les législateurs Français doivent s'occuper de l'éducation publique autrement que pour en protéger les progrès, et si la constitution la plus favorable au développement du *moi humain*, et les lois les plus propres à mettre chacun à sa place, ne sont pas la seule éducation que le peuple doive attendre d'eux," *l. c.* p. 11. "D'après cela, les principes rigoureux scmbleraient exiger que l'Assemblée Nationale ne s'occupât de l'éducation que pour l'enlever à des pouvoirs ou à des corps qui peuvent en dépraver l'influence," *l. c.* p. 12.

# CHAPTER VII.

## RELIGION.

BESIDES that education of the young to which our attention has just been directed, there is another important means for exercising an influence on the morals and character of a nation, through which the State endeavours to educate, as it were, the full-grown man, accompanies him throughout the whole course and conduct of his life—his ways of thinking and acting,—and aims at imparting to them some definite and preconceived direction, or forestalling probable deviations from the path it prescribes;—this is Religion.

History shows us that all States have thought fit to avail themselves of this source of influence, but with very different designs, and in very different degrees. In the ancient nations it was perfectly interwoven with the political constitution,—it was, in fact, a grand guiding principle and essential pillar of the State organism; and hence all that I have observed of similar ancient institutions, applies no less aptly to religion. When the Christian religion, instead of the earlier local deities of nations, taught men to believe in a universal God of humanity, thereby throwing down one of the most dangerous barriers which sundered the different tribes of the great human family from each other;—and when it thus succeeded in laying the foundation for all true human virtue, human development, and human union, without which, enlightenment and even science and learning would have long, and perhaps always, remained the rare property of a few;—it also directly operated to loosen the strong bond of connection that of old existed between religion and the political constitution. But when, afterwards, the incursion of the barbarian tribes had scared enlightenment away;—when a misconception of that very religion inspired a blind and intolerant rage for proselytism; and when, at the same time, the political form of States underwent such changes, that citizens were transformed into subjects, and these not so much the subjects of the State as of the person in whom the government was vested;—the solicitude for religion, its preservation and extension, was left to the conscientiousness of princes, who believed it confided to their hands by God himself. In our times this prejudice has, comparatively, ceased to prevail; but the promotion of religion by laws and State institutions has been no less urgently recommended by considerations of internal security, and of morality, its strongest bulwark. These, then, I regard as the principal distinctive epochs in the history of religion as a political element, although I am not prepared to deny that all these reasons, characteristic of each, and especially the last-mentioned, have been co-operating throughout, while at each period, doubtless, one of them prevailed.

In the endeavour to act upon morality through the medium of religious ideas, it is especially necessary to distinguish between the propagation of a certain form of religion, and the diffusion of a spirit of religiousness in general. The former is undoubtedly more oppressive in its character, and more hurtful in its consequences; but, without it, the latter is hardly possible. For when once the State believes morality and religiousness to be inseparably associated, and considers that it can and may avail itself of this method of influence, it is scarcely possible, so long as there are various forms of religious opinion,—corresponding differently with morality, whether true, or constructed

E

according to accepted notions,—that it should not extend
its protection to one of these forms of religion in preference to the others.   Even where it aims at wholly avoiding
this preference, and assumes the position of protector or
defender of all religious parties, it can only judge of what
it defends from external actions, and must therefore indirectly countenance the opinions of those parties who actually come under its cognizance, to the suppression of other
possible but unmanifested varieties of belief; and in any
case, it evinces its concern for one opinion at least, in that
it strives to render the real, living belief in a God the one
generally predominant.   It will be evident, moreover, on a
moment's reflection,—and the consideration is especially important in regard to what we would maintain,—that, owing
to the vagueness and ambiguity of all expressions, which
enable them to convey so many different ideas by the same
general word, the State itself would be obliged to supply
some definite interpretation of the term Religiousness, before it could apply it in any way as a clear rule of conduct.
So that I would absolutely deny the possibility of any
State interference in religious affairs which should not be
more or less chargeable with encouraging certain distinct
opinions, and did not therefore admit the application of
principles and arguments, derivable from the supposition of
such a partial tendency.   Neither, with any more reason,
can I grant the possibility of any such interference, without
the implication of some guiding and controlling influence—
some drag and hindrance, as it were, upon the liberty of
the individual.   For, however widely certain kinds of influence may naturally differ from coercion,—as exhortation,
or the mere procuring of facilities for the acceptance of
ideas,—there still exists, even in the last of these (as we
have already tried to demonstrate more fully in the case of
several similar institutions), a certain preponderance of the

State's views, which is calculated to repress and diminish freedom.

I have thought it necessary to make these preliminary observations, in order to anticipate an objection that might, perhaps, be advanced as I proceed, viz. that in the views I entertain of the consequences of a solicitude for religion, my attention was confined to the encouragement of certain particular forms, to the exclusion of the possibility of a care for religion in general; and I hoped moreover thus to avoid needlessly embarrassing and dismembering my inquiry, by a too minute review of the single possible cases.

All religion,—viewing it in its relation to morality and happiness, and as it has therefore become a matter of feeling,—rests upon a want or necessity of the soul. It is obvious that in thus restricting my view, I am not considering religion in so far as reason perceives, or fancies it perceives, any religious truth; for the perception of truth is independent of all influence from the will or desire;—nor in so far as revelation tends to strengthen any particular belief; since even historical belief should be exempt from all such influences derived from our sensitive nature. We hope, we dread, because we desire. Wherever there is no vestige of spiritual culture, this want or necessity is purely sensuous in its character. Fear and hope with regard to the phenomena of external nature, which are transformed by fancy into spiritual existences, constitute the whole sum of religion. But when culture dawns on the spirit, this is no longer sufficient and satisfying. The soul then yearns towards an intuition of perfection, of which a scintillation faintly glimmers in itself, but whose clear, complete effulgence, a deep presentiment assures it, is without. This first intuition gradually merges into admiration; and conceiving of himself as in some relation to this higher existence, man's wonder ripens into love, from which there springs a longing to assimilate himself to this outward manifestation of perfection,—a desire for union. This development of the religious idea is even true of nations in the lowest grade of civilization; for it is from this very process of conception that, even among the rudest tribes, the chiefs of the people are brought to believe themselves lineally descended from the gods, and destined, after death, to return to them. It is only to be observed that the actual conception of the Divine Nature varies according to the different ideas of perfection which prevail in particular ages and nations. The gods of the remoter ages of Greece and Rome, and those worshiped by our own earliest forefathers, were simply ideals of bodily strength and prowess. When to this view of perfection the idea of sensuous beauty succeeded and gradually became refined, the sensuous personification of beauty was exalted to the throne of Deity; and hence arose what we would designate as the Religion of Art. Further, when men ascended from the sensuous to the purely spiritual— from the beautiful to the good and true, the sum of all moral and intellectual perfection became the high object of their adoration, and religion the property of philosophy. It might perhaps be possible to estimate the comparative worth of the different forms of religion that have prevailed according to this ascending scale, if it were true that religion varied according to nations and sects, and not according to the nature of single individuals. But, as it is, religion is wholly subjective, and depends solely on the manner of individual conception.

When the idea formed of Divinity is the fruit of true spiritual culture, its intimate re-action on the inner perfection is at once beneficial and beautiful. All things assume a new form and meaning in our eyes when regarded as the creatures of forecasting design, and not the capricious handiwork of unreasoning chance. The ideas of wisdom

order, and adaptative forethought,—ideas so necessary to
the conduct of our own actions, and even to the culture of
the intellect,—strike deeper root into our susceptible nature, when we discover them everywhere around us. The
finite becomes, as it were, infinite; the perishable, enduring; the fleeting, stable; the complex, simple,—when we
contemplate one great regulating Cause on the summit of
things, and regard what is spiritual as endlessly enduring.
Our search after truth, our striving after perfection, gain
greater certainty and consistency when we can believe
in the existence of a Being who is at once the source of
all truth, and the sum of all perfection. The soul becomes less painfully sensible of the chances and changes
of fortune, when it learns how to connect hope and confidence with such calamities. The feeling of receiving
everything we possess from the hand of love, tends no less
to exalt our moral excellence and enhance our happiness.
Through a constant sense of gratitude for enjoyment—
through clinging with fond trustfulness to the object towards which it yearns, the soul is drawn out of itself, nor
always broods in jealous isolation over its own sensations,
its own plans, hopes, and fears. Should it lose the exalting
feeling of owing everything to itself, it still enjoys the
rapture of living in the love of another,—a feeling in which
its own perfection is united with the perfection of that
other being. It becomes disposed to be to others what
others are to it; it would not that they too should receive
nothing but from themselves, in the same way that it receives nothing from others. I have ventured to touch, in
these remarks, on the subject of the co-operation of religion with morality; to enter into it more fully, after the
masterly exposition of Garve,* would be at once useless and
presuming.

---

* Humboldt appears to refer to the Essay " Ueber das Dasein Gottes," in

But although the influence of religious ideas unmistakably harmonizes and co-operates with the process of moral perfection, it is no less certain that such ideas are in no way inseparably associated with that process. The simple idea of moral perfection is great, and inspiring, and exalted enough to require no other veil or form ; and every religion is based on personification to a greater or less degree, —represents itself in some shape of appeal to the senses,— some or other modification of anthropomorphism. The idea of perfection will still hover before him who has not been wont to comprise the sum of all moral excellence in one absolute Ideal, and to conceive of himself as in a relation with that being : it will be to him at once the grand incentive to all activity, and the element of all his happiness. Firmly assured by experience of the possibility of raising his soul to a higher degree of moral perfection, he will strive with earnest and unwearying efforts to reach the goal he has set before him. The thought of the possible annihilation of his being will cease to alarm, when his illusive imagination is no longer painfully alive to the sense of nothingness in the non-existence of death. His unalterable dependency on the capricious mutations of fortune no more daunts and dismays him : comparatively indifferent to external joys and privations, he regards only what is purely moral and intellectual ; and no mere freak of changeful destiny has power to disturb the calm, inner life of his soul. His spirit is exalted to a proud height of independence through its perfect sense of self-sufficingness—its lofty superiority to external vicissitude—the rich and overflowing fulness of its own ideas—the profound consciousness of its internal, deep-seated strength. And then when he looks back to his eventful journey in the past, and retraces its onward progress, step by step, through doubt and difficulty;

Garve's ' Versuche über verschiedene Gegenstände aus der Moral, der Literatur, und dem gesellschaftlichen Leben.' (Breslau, 1792–1800. 5 vols. 8vo.)

when he sees with what varied means and happy appli-
ances every separate circumstance was made so happily
focal to the whole, and with what a regular series of gradations he arrived at that which he now is; when he learns
to perceive in himself the complete union of cause and
effect, of end and means, and, full of the noblest pride of
which finite beings are capable, exclaims,

> " Hast not thyself accomplished all,
> Thou heart with holy ardour glowing ?"*

how will dark and despairing thoughts—the thoughts of
his lonely and unsolaced life—of helplessness, of failing support and consolation, vanish from before him,—thoughts
which we are wont to believe mostly to beset those in whose
minds the idea of a personal, superintending, rational cause
of the chain of finite being is wanting! This constant,
ruling self-consciousness, moreover, this living solely in and
through himself, need not render the moral man callous and
insensible to the lot and happiness of others, or shut out
from his heart every loving sympathy and benevolent impulse.
This very idea of perfection, towards which all his activity
converges as to a grand, sufficient centre, so far from being a
mere cold abstraction of the reason, may prove a warm and
genial feeling of the heart, and thus transport his existence
into the existence of others. For in them too there exists
a like capacity for greater perfection, and this latent fitness
it may be in his power to elicit and improve. He is not
yet penetrated with the loftiest idea of all morality, so long
as he can be content to regard himself or others as distinct
and isolated—so long as all spiritual existences seem not to
him merged and united in the sum of perfection which lies
diffused around him. Nay, his union with other beings

---

* " Hast du nicht alles selbst vollendet,
Heilig, glühend Herz ?"—Goethe, Prometheus, II. 63.

of kindred nature with himself is perhaps only the more intimate, and his sympathy in their fates and fortunes only the more keen and constant, in proportion as their destiny and his own seem to him to be entirely dependent on him and them.

If it is objected to this picture (and it is an objection which might fairly be urged) that to realize it in actual life would be a task far beyond the common range of human energy and capability, I would reply that such a condition is no less essential in order that religious feelings become the groundwork, in a man's character, of a truly beautiful life, equally removed from coldness on the one hand and enthusiasm on the other. The force of this objection could only be admitted, moreover, if I had peculiarly recommended the cultivation of that harmony of being which I have just endeavoured to portray. But, as it is, my only object was to show that human morality, even the highest and most consistent, is not at all dependent on religion, or in general necessarily connected with it, and haply to contribute a few collateral reasons for removing the faintest shadow of spiritual intolerance, and for cherishing that profound respect which we should ever entertain for the individual thoughts and feelings of our fellow-men. If it were necessary still further to justify the view thus taken of morality, it were easy to delineate a contrasting picture of the pernicious influences of which an exclusive religious disposition, as well as its opposite, are capable. But it is painful to dwell on such ungrateful themes, and history only supplies us too abundantly with convincing illustrations. It may be more conducive to our present design, and furnish us a greater weight of evidence in favour of the principles we advocate, to cast a hasty glance at the nature of morality itself, and at the close relation of religious systems, as well as of religiousness, to the system of human sensation.

Now, neither that which morality prescribes as a duty, nor that which gives sanction to its dictates and recommends them to the will, is dependent on religious ideas. I will not dwell on the consideration that such a dependency would even impair the purity of the moral will. In reasoning derived from experience, and to be similarly referred to it, this position might not be thought sufficiently valid. But the qualities of an action which constitute it a duty, arise partly from the very nature of the human soul, and partly from the stricter reference to men's mutual relations; and, although it is certain that these qualities are especially recommended and enhanced by a feeling of religion, this is neither the sole medium of impressing them on the heart, nor by any means one which admits of application to every variety of character. On the contrary, religion depends wholly for its efficiency on the individual nature, and is, in the strictest acceptation, subjective. The man whose character is cold and essentially reflective—whose conception never passes into sensation—with whom it is enough to see clearly the natural tendency of things to shape his resolution accordingly, needs no religious motive to induce him to adopt a course of virtuous action, and, as far as is consistent with such a form of character, to be virtuous. But it is wholly otherwise in the opposite case, where the capacity of sensation is peculiarly strong, and every thought rapidly merges in feeling. And yet even here the shades and modifications of character are infinitely various. For example, wherever the soul feels a strong and resistless impulse to pass out from itself, and establish a union with others, religious ideas will prove genuine and efficient motives. But, on the other hand, there are varieties of character in which so intimate a sequence prevails between all feeling and ideas— which share such a profundity of conception and sensation, that they acquire a measure of strength and self-reliance

E 3

which neither needs nor allows the surrender of the whole nature to another being, and cannot entertain that confidence in foreign strength in which religion especially manifests itself. The very circumstances, even, which dispose the soul to revert to ideas of religion, assume a different significance from this same diversity of character. With one, every powerful emotion, every impulse to joy or sorrow, suffices; with another, the simple and spontaneous outflow of gratitude for enjoyment. Perhaps such a disposition as this to which we have last referred, is far from being the least estimable. While those whom it characterizes have a confident strength of their own, which does not urge them to look for external help in trial and misfortune, they have, on the other hand, too keen a sense of the feeling of being loved, not to associate with the idea of enjoyment the endearing image of a loving benefactor. The longing for religious ideas, moreover, has often a still nobler, purer, and, so to speak, a still more intellectual source. Whatever man beholds in the world around him, he perceives only through the medium of the senses; the pure essence is nowhere immediately revealed to his gaze; even that which inspires him with the most ardent love and enthusiasm, and takes the strongest hold on his whole nature, is mysteriously shrouded in the densest veil. There are some minds to which this sentiment is most constantly and vividly present; the engrossing object of their lifelong activity is a striving to penetrate this mysterious vesture,— their whole pleasure, a presentiment of truth in the enigma which is enwrapped in the symbol—a hope of uninterruptedly contemplating it in other periods of existence. Now it is when, in wonderful and beautiful harmony, the spirit is thus restlessly searching, and the heart fondly yearning, for this immediate contemplation of the actual existence— when the scantiness of conception does not suffice to the deep force of thought, nor the shadowy image of fancy and the senses, to the living warmth of feeling,—it is then that belief uninterruptedly follows the peculiar bent of reason to enlarge every conception beyond all barriers between itself and the ideal, and that it clings closely to the idea of a Being which comprehends all other beings, and, purely and without medium, exists, contemplates, and creates. But, on the other hand, in some minds a prudent diffidence serves to confine belief within the domain of experience: often, it is true, the feeling willingly delights in the contemplation of the ideal so peculiar to reason, but finds a more pleasurable fascination in the endeavour to interweave the sensuous and spiritual natures in a closer union—to lend a richer significance to the symbol, and render it a more intelligible and suggestive embodiment of the truth; and thus man is often compensated for the loss of that enthusiasm of hopeful longing, by that ever-attendant consciousness of the success of his endeavours which strictly forbids his gaze to wander lost in endless distances. Though less bold, his course is more certain; the conception of reason to which he closely clings is still clearer; the sensuous intuition, although a less faithful reflex of the truth, is more readily adapted to experience, and therefore more fully answers his requirements. On the whole, there is nothing which the mind so willingly admires, and is inclined to with such perfect unison of feeling, as the recognition of orderful omniscience presiding in a countless number of various and even antagonistic individuals. Yet this admiration is far more characteristic of some minds than others; and there are some who more readily embrace a belief according to which one Being created and regulated the universe, and ever preserves it with the solicitude of far-seeing wisdom. In the conception of others, the individual seems more sacred; they are more peculiarly attracted by this idea than

by the universality of adaptative order; and to such minds an
opposite system is usually suggested, that, namely, in which
the individual essence, developing itself in itself, and subject
to the modification of reciprocal influences, becomes attuned
to that perfect harmony of being in which alone the human
heart and mind can find repose.    I am far from supposing
that I have exhausted in these insufficient sketches a subject which is so copious as to defy all methodical investigation.  My only object has been to show, by a few illustrative
examples, that not only all true religiousness, but every true
system of religion, proceeds, in the highest sense, from the
innermost harmony and correlation of man's processes of
sensation.

Now, it is doubtless true, that the conceptions of design,
order, correspondency, and perfection, or all that is purely
*intellectual* in religious ideas, is wholly independent of peculiar methods of sensation or the necessary differences of
character. But while we allow this, it becomes us to add that
we are not now regarding these ideas in the abstract, but
rather in their influence on men, who do not preserve that
independency in the same degree; and to observe further,
that such ideas are not by any means the exclusive property
of religion.   The idea of perfection is at first derived from
our impressions of animate nature, and, thence transferred
to the inanimate, it approaches, step by step, to the all-
perfect, stripped of every barrier.    But does not nature
remain the same also for the contemplation of the moral
man, and might it not be possible to advance through all the
preceding gradations of approach, and still to pause before
the last?  Now, if all religiousness depends so absolutely on
the varied phases and modifications of character, and more
particularly of feeling, the influence it exercises on morality
cannot be based on the sum and substance of accepted dogmas, but on the peculiar form of their acceptance—on con-

viction and belief. I shall have occasion hereafter to apply this conclusion to other important considerations, and I
trust it may be reasonably admitted from what I have here
observed. The only reproach, perhaps, to which my treatment of this entire question may fairly be open, is that I
have confined my views to men who are favoured alike by
nature and by circumstances, and are for that reason so rare,
while they interest us so deeply. But I hope to show in the
sequel that I am far from overlooking the masses of which
society is mainly composed, while I would observe, meanwhile, that it strikes me as unworthy of a noble mind to
proceed from any but the loftiest premises, whenever human
nature is the subject of inquiry.

If, after these general considerations on religion, and the
nature of its influence in human life, I now return to the
question whether the State should employ it as a means for
reforming the morals of its citizens, it will be granted that
the methods adopted by the legislator for the promotion of
moral culture are always correspondent with their proposed
end, and efficient in their practical working, according as
they cherish the internal development of capacities and inclinations. For all moral growth and culture spring solely
and immediately from the inner life of the soul, and can
only be *induced* in human nature, and never produced by
mere external and artificial contrivances. Now, it is unquestionable, that religion, which is wholly based on ideas,
sensations, and internal convictions, affords precisely such
a means of disposing and influencing a man's nature from
within. We develope the artist by accustoming his eye to
dwell on the grand masterpieces of artistic skill; we expand his imagination by a study of the faultlessly beautiful
models of antiquity; and in like manner must the process
of moral development be effected through the contemplation
of loftier moral perfection, in the school of social intercourse,

in the mirror of past history, and lastly in the contemplation of its sublimest ideal in the image of Divinity itself. And yet, as I have already shown, this last glimpse of moral perfection is scarcely designed for every eye, or rather, to abandon metaphor, this manner of conception is only adapted to certain varieties of character. But even although this method of self-development were universally possible, it would only be efficient when grounded on the perfect coherency of all ideas and sensations, or when unfolded from the inner life of the soul, rather than imposed on it or importunately suggested by some external influence. Hence it will appear that the only means by which the legislator can attain the end in view, must be by removing obstacles that prevent the citizen's mind from becoming familiarized with religious ideas, and by promoting a spirit of free inquiry. If, proceeding further, he ventures to direct or diffuse a spirit of religiousness; if he shelters or encourages certain definite religious ideas ; or if, lastly, he dares to require a belief according to authority in lieu of a true and sincere conviction, he will most effectually thwart and deaden the soul's noblest aspirations, and throw fatal impediments in the way of true spiritual culture ; and, although he so far work on the citizen's imagination by immediate emotions as to succeed in bringing his actions into conformity with the law, he can never produce true virtue. For this is independent of all peculiar forms of religious belief, and incompatible with any that is enjoined by, and believed on, authority.

Still, however, the question arises, If the influence of certain religious principles tends to produce and encourage those actions only which harmonize with the requirements of law, is this not enough to entitle the State to see to their diffusion, even at the sacrifice of general freedom of thought? The State's design is surely fully accomplished when its legal

injunctions are strictly observed; and the legislator seems
to have adequately discharged his duty when he has succeeded in framing wise laws, and seen how to secure their
authority with the citizen. The idea of virtue, moreover,
which has just been enunciated, is only true of a few classes
of the political community, of those, namely, whose position
enables them to devote their time and means to the process
of internal development. The State has to embrace the
majority in the circle of its solicitude, and these are manifestly incapable of that higher degree of morality.

It would be a sufficient answer to this reasoning, and
serve to remove the ground from the objection which it
suggests, to oppose the principle established in the former
portion of this essay—that the State institution is not in
itself an end, but is only a means towards human development; and hence, that it is not enough for the legislator to succeed in investing his dictates with authority,
so long as the means through which that authority operates
are not at the same time good, or, at least, innocuous. But
apart from this fundamental principle, it is erroneous to
suppose that the citizen's actions and their legal propriety
are only important as far as the State is concerned. A State
is such a complex and intricate machine, that its laws, which
must always be few in number, and simple and general in
their nature, cannot possibly prove adequate to the full accomplishment of its ends. The great essentials for social
welfare are always left to be secured by the voluntary and
harmonious endeavours of the citizens. To exhibit this, it
is only necessary to contrast the prosperity and ample resources of a cultivated and enlightened people, with the
wants and deficiencies of any ruder and less civilized community. It is for this reason that all who have occupied
themselves with political affairs, have invariably been animated with the design of rendering the well-being of the

State the direct, personal interest of the citizen. They have laboured to bring the political organism into the condition of a machine, which should always be preserved in its highest efficiency by the inner force and vitality of its springs, so as not to require the continual application of fresh external influences. Indeed, if modern States can lay claim to any marked superiority over those of antiquity, it is chiefly in the fact that they have more fully and clearly realized this principle. That they have done so, the very circumstance of their employing religion as a means of culture is a striking proof. But still, even religion, in so far as it is designed to produce good actions alone, by the faithful observance of certain positive principles, or to exercise a positive influence on morals in general,—even religion is a foreign agency, and operates only from without. Hence it should always remain the ultimate object of the legislator—an object which a perfect knowledge of human nature will convince him is attainable only by granting the highest degree of freedom— to elevate the culture of the citizen to such a point, that he may find every incentive to co-operation in the State's designs, in the consciousness of the advantages which the political institution affords him for the immediate furtherance of his individual schemes and interests. Now, that such an understanding should prevail, implies the diffusion of enlightenment and a high degree of mental culture; and these can never flourish or spread themselves where the spirit of free inquiry is fettered and impeded by laws.

Meanwhile, the propriety and expediency of such extensions of State agency are only acknowledged, because the conviction maintains its ground that neither external tranquillity nor morality can be secured without generally-received religious principles, or, at least, without the State's supervision of the citizen's religion, and that without these it would be impossible to preserve the authority of the law.

Still, however prevalent this belief may be, it seems to me necessary to institute some more careful and searching investigation into the influence exercised by religious dogmas thus received, and indeed by any manifestation of a religious spirit called forth by political institutions. Now, as regards the acceptance of religious truth by the less cultivated masses of the people, most reliance is to be reposed in the ideas of future rewards and punishments. But these do nothing to lessen the propensity to immoral actions, or strengthen the leaning to that which is good, and therefore cannot improve the character: they simply work on the imagination, and therefore influence action as do images of fancy in general; but that influence is in like manner dissipated and destroyed by all that impairs the force and vivacity of the imaginative faculty. If we remember, moreover, that even in the minds of the most faithful believers these expectations are so remote, and therefore so uncertain, that they lose much of their efficiency from the thoughts of subsequent reformation, of future repentance, of hopes of pardon, which are so much encouraged by certain religious conceptions, it will be difficult for us to conceive how such tenets can do more to influence conduct than the sure consciousness of civil punishments, which, with good police arrangements, are near and certain in their operation, and are not to be averted by any possibility of repentance or subsequent reformation. Provided only that the citizen were familiarized with the retributive certainty of these punishments from his childhood, and taught to trace the consequences of moral and immoral actions, we cannot suppose such present influences to be less effectual than the other remote ideas.

But, on the other hand, it is not to be doubted that even comparatively unenlightened conceptions of religion often manifest themselves in far nobler and higher views of duty,

in the case of a large portion of the people. The thought
of being an object of affectionate solicitude to an all-wise
and perfect Being, imparts new dignity to the character;
the trust in endless duration leads the soul to loftier views,
and infuses a spirit of order and design into the actions;
the feeling of the loving goodness of Deity imbues the heart
of the believer with a kindred disposition; and, in short, religion tends to inspire men's souls with a sense of the
beauty of virtue. But wherever such fair dispositions as
these are expected to follow in the train of religion, the
religious sentiment must be infused into the whole system
of thought and sensation; and we cannot conceive this possible where the spirit of free inquiry is prostrated and enfeebled, and everything is reduced to a mere passive belief:
before such results could arrive, moreover, there must have
been some latent sense of better feelings, which must be
taken as an undeveloped tendency towards morality, and on
which the religious sentiment afterwards reacted. And, on
the whole, no one will be disposed to utterly deny the influence of religion on morality; the only question at issue
is, whether that influence reposes on a few religious dogmas,
and, secondly, whether it is such as to show an indissoluble
union between them. Both suppositions I hold to be erroneous. Virtue harmonizes so sweetly and naturally with
man's original inclinations; the feelings of love, of social
concord, of justice, have in them something so dear and
prepossessing, those of disinterested effort, of self-sacrifice,
something so sublime and ennobling, and the thousand relations which grow out of these feelings in domestic and
social life contribute so largely to human happiness, that
it is far less necessary to look for new incentives to virtuous
action, than simply to secure for those already implanted in
the soul a more free and unhindered operation. Should we
however be disposed to go further, and endeavour to supply

new and additional encouragements to a moral course of life, we should not forget, through a spirit of one-sidedness, to strike the balance between their useful and hurtful tendencies. After so much has been said of the pernicious results arising from restricted freedom of thought, it hardly seems necessary to enforce this caution by any circumstantial exposition, and I have, besides, already dwelt sufficiently, in the former part of this chapter, on the hurtfulness of all positive promotion of religiousness by the State. If those injurious consequences of restriction were confined merely to the results of the inquiries—if they occasioned nothing more than incompleteness or inexactness in our scientific knowledge, we might proceed, with some show of reason, to estimate the advantages which might perhaps be justly expected to flow from such a policy. But, as it is, the danger is far more serious. The importance of free inquiry extends to our whole manner of thinking, and even acting. He who is accustomed to judge of truth and error without regard to external relations, either as affecting himself or others, and to hear them so discussed, is able to realize principles of action more calmly and consistently, and with more exclusive reference to loftier points of view, than one whose reflections are constantly influenced by a variety of circumstances not essential to the subject under investigation. Inquiry, as well as conviction, the result to which it leads, is spontaneity; while belief is reliance on some foreign power, some external perfection, moral or intellectual. Hence it is that firmness and self-dependence are such striking characteristics of the thoughtful inquirer, while a corresponding weakness and inaction seem to mark the confiding believer. It is true, that where belief has stifled every form of doubt and gained the supreme mastery, it often creates a far more irresistible courage and extraordinary spirit of defiant endurance, as we see in the history of all enthusiasts; but this kind of energy is never desirable except when some definite external result is in question, which requires such a machine-like activity for its accomplishment; and it is wholly inapplicable in cases which imply individual decision, deliberate actions grounded on principles of reason, and, above all, internal perfection. Of this we shall be convinced when we remember, that the strength which supports such enthusiasm is wholly dependent on the suppression of all activity in the powers of reason. To continue: doubt is torture to the believer only, and not to him who follows the results of his own inquiries; for, to the latter, results are in general far less important. During the process of inquiry, he becomes conscious of his soul's activity, its inherent strength; he feels that his perfection, his happiness, depend upon this strength; and instead of being oppressed by his doubts concerning the principles he conceived to be true, he congratulates himself that his increasing force of thought enables him to see clearly through errors that had till now remained hidden. The believer, on the contrary, is only interested in the result itself, for, the truth once perceived, there is nothing further to be sought for. The doubts which reason arouses afflict and depress him, for they are no longer, as in the case of one who thinks for himself, new means for arriving at the truth; they only serve to rob him of certainty without revealing any other method of recovering it. If we were to follow out these suggestive considerations, we should be led to observe that it is in general wrong to attribute so much importance to single inferences or results, and to suppose that either so many other truths, or so many useful consequences, internal and external, are necessarily dependent on their implicit acceptance. It is from such a fatal misconception that the course of inquiry so often comes to a stand-still, and that the most free and enlightened conclusions seem to react against the very basis on which alone they have arisen. Hence it is that freedom of thought assumes such vital importance, and anything that tends to limit or repress its natural exercise is so fatally injurious.

Again, if we regard the question in another aspect, the State has no want of means for enforcing the authority of its laws, and preventing the commission of crime. Let the governing power do its best to close up such sources of immoral actions as are to be found in the State constitution itself; let it quicken the vigilant activity of the police with regard to crimes actually perpetrated; let it attend to the udicious infliction of punishment, and the desired end will be effectually secured. It cannot surely be forgotten, that freedom of thought, and the enlightenment which never flourishes but beneath its shelter, are the most efficient of all means for promoting security. While all other methods are confined to the mere suppression of actual outbreaks, free inquiry acts immediately on the very dispositions and sentiments; and while those only serve to maintain due order and propriety in external actions, this creates an internal harmony between the will and the endeavour. When shall we learn, moreover, to set less value on the mere visible results of actions, than on the temper and disposition of soul from which they flow? When will one arise to accomplish for legislation what Rousseau gained for education, and draw our attention from mere external, physical results, to the internal life and development of the soul?

In estimating the advantages arising from increased freedom of thought and the consequent wide diffusion of enlightenment, we should moreover especially guard against presuming that they would be confined to a small proportion of the people only;—that to the majority, whose energies are exhausted by cares for the physical necessaries of life, such opportunities would be useless or even positively hurtful, and that the only way to influence the masses is to promulgate some definite points of belief—to restrict the freedom of thought. There is something degrading to human nature in the idea of refusing to any man, the right to be a man. There are none so hopelessly low on the scale of culture and refinement as to be incapable of rising higher; and even though the more pure and lofty views of philosophy and religion could not at once be entertained by a large portion of the community—though it should be necessary to array truth in some different garb before it could find admission to their convictions—should we have to appeal rather to their feeling and imagination than to the cold decision of reason, still, the diffusiveness imparted to all scientific knowledge by freedom and enlightenment spreads gradually downward even to them; and the happy results of perfect liberty of thought on the mind and character of the entire nation, extend their influence even to its humblest individuals.

In order to give a more general character to this reasoning (mainly directed, as it is, to political solicitude for the propagation of certain religious doctrines), I have yet to adduce the principle before established, that all influence of religion on morality depends especially, if not entirely, on the form in which the religious sentiment exists in the individual man, and not on the peculiar tenour of the doctrines which make it sacred in his eyes. Now, all State institutions, as I also before maintained, act solely on the substance of the doctrines in a greater or less degree; whilst as regards the form of their acceptance by the individual, the channels of influence are wholly closed to any political agency. The way in which religion springs up in the human heart, and the way in which it is received in each case, depend entirely on the whole manner of the man's existence—the whole system of his thoughts and sensations. But, if the State *were* able to remodel these according to its views (a possibility which we can hardly conceive), I must have been very unfortunate in the exposition of my principles if it were necessary to re-establish the conclusion which meets this remote possibility, viz., that the State may not make man an instrument to subserve its arbitrary designs, and induce him to neglect for these his proper individual ends. And that there is no absolute necessity, such as would perhaps alone justify an exception in this instance, is apparent from that perfect independence of morality on religion which I have already sought to establish, but which will receive a stronger confirmation when I show that the preservation of a State's internal security, does not at all require that a proper and distinct direction should be given to the national morals in general. Now, if there is one thing more calculated than another to prepare a fertile soil for religion in the minds of the citizens,—if there is anything to cause that religion which has been infused into the system of thought and sensation to react beneficially on morality, it is freedom, which always (even though it be in the slightest degree) suffers from the exercise of a positive solicitude on the part of the State. For the greater the diversity and characteristic peculiarity of man's development, and the more sublime his feeling, the more easily does he recall his gaze from the narrow, changing circle that surrounds him, and turn to that whose infinity and unity include the reason of those limits and the method of that change,—whether he may hope to realize such a conception of Divinity or not. The greater a man's freedom, the more does he become dependent on himself, and well-disposed towards others. Now, nothing leads us so directly to Deity as benevolent love; and nothing renders the absence of a living belief in God so harmless as self-reliant power—self-sufficing and self-contained. Finally, the higher the feeling of power in man, and the more free and unimpeded its manifestation, the more willingly does he seek to discover some internal bond to lead and direct him; and thus he remains attached to morality, whether this bond is to him a feeling of reverence and love for the Divinity, or the earnest and recompense of his own self-consciousness.

The difference, then, appears to me to be this :—the citizen who is wholly left to himself in matters of religion will, or will not, interweave religious feelings with his inner life, according to his individual character ; but, in either case, his system of ideas will be more coherent, and his impressions deeper ; there will be more perfect oneness in his being, and so he will be more uniformly disposed to morality and obedience to the laws. On the other hand, he who is fettered by various restrictive institutions will, despite of these, entertain different religious ideas or not, subject to the same modifying influences ; but, in either case, he will possess less sequence of ideas, less depth and sincerity of feeling, less harmony and oneness of being, and so will have less regard for morality, and wish more frequently to evade the operation of the laws.

Hence, then, without adducing any further reasons, I may safely proceed to lay down the principle, by no means a novel one, *that all which concerns religion lies beyond the sphere of the State's activity; and that the choice of ministers, as well as all that relates to religious worship in general, should be left to the free judgment of the communities, without any special supervision on the part of the State.*

# CHAPTER VIII.

## AMELIORATION OF MORALS.

THE last means which States are wont to employ, in order to reform the moral condition of the nation correspondently with their design of maintaining security, is the influence of special laws and enactments. But as these cannot be made to induce any direct disposition towards virtue and morality, it manifestly follows that special provisions of this nature can do nothing more than prohibit particular actions of the citizens, or mark out those which, without directly infringing on the rights of others, are either positively immoral or are likely to lead to immorality.

To this class of institutions all sumptuary laws especially belong. For, it is evident, there is no such common and fruitful source of immoral, and even lawless actions, as an excessive propensity of the soul towards the sensual, or the disproportion subsisting between desires and impulses in general, and the powers of satisfaction which the external position affords. When there exists a general spirit of continence and moderation, which serves to reconcile men to their allotted sphere, they are not so strongly impelled to transgress its limits to the infraction of another's rights, or, at least, to do anything likely to disturb their own happiness and contentment.

Hence it would seem to be strictly consistent with the true end of the State, to confine sensualism within due bounds, since it is the essential source from which all collisions between man and man proceed (for that in which the

F

spiritual prevails can always, and in all cases, subsist in harmony) ; and further, because it would appear the simplest and easiest method of effecting that object, it might be argued that the State should endeavour, as far as possible, to suppress sensualism altogether.

Still, to adhere faithfully to the principle which has hitherto guided us in this investigation—viz. first of all to regard any proposed means of State agency in the light of man's true and unmistakable interests,—it becomes us to inquire into the influence of sensualism on human life, development, activity, and happiness, so far as concerns our present purpose; and while such an investigation will naturally lead us to portray the innermost nature of the acting and enjoying man, it will serve at the same time to illustrate more graphically the hurtful or beneficial consequences which flow in general from restrictions imposed on freedom. It is only after such a radical inquiry that we can be in a position to decide as to the State's competence to act positively on morals, and so arrive at the solution of this part of the general question we have proposed.

The impressions, inclinations, and passions which have their immediate source in the senses, are those which first and most violently manifest themselves in human nature. Wherever, before the refining influences of culture have imparted a new direction to the soul's energies, these impressions, etc., do not show themselves, all seeds of power have perished, and nothing either good or great can take root and flourish. They constitute the great original source of all spontaneous activity, and first inspire a glowing, genial warmth in human nature. They infuse life and elastic vigour into the soul: when unsatisfied, they render it active, buoyant, ingenious in the invention of schemes, and courageous in their execution; when satisfied, they promote an easy and unhindered play of ideas. In general, they animate and quicken all conceptions with a greater and more varied activity, suggest new views, point out hitherto unnoticed aspects, and, according to the manner in which they are satisfied, intimately react on the physical organization, which in its turn acts upon the soul, although we only notice how from the results.

The influence, however, of these impressions and inclinations differs, not only in its intensity, but in the manner of its operation. This is, to a certain extent, owing to their strength or weakness; but it is also partly to be attributed to their degree of affinity with the spiritual element in human nature, or from the difficulty or facility of raising them from mere animal gratifications to human pleasures. Thus, for instance, the eye imparts to the substance of its impressions that outline of form which is so full of enjoyment and fertile in ideas; while the ear lends to sound the proportionate succession of tones in the order of time. The nature of these impressions readily suggests many interesting reflections, if this were the proper place for such a topic, but I will only pause to notice their different importance as regards the culture of the soul.

The eye supplies the reason, so to speak, with a more prepared substance; and the inner part of our nature, with its own form and that of other things which stand in a relation to it, is thus presented to us in a single and distinct situation. If we conceive of the ear merely as an organ of sense, and in so far as it does not receive and communicate words, it conveys far less distinctness of impression. And it is for this reason that Kant assigns the preference to the plastic arts when compared with music. But he observes that the culture secured to the soul by the several arts, (and I would add, directly secured,) is presupposed as a scale for determining this preference.

The question, however, presents itself whether this scale

of previous culture is the just standard of appreciation. Energy appears to me to be the first and chiefest of human virtues. Whatever exalts our energy is of greater worth than aught that merely puts materials into our hands for its exercise. Now, as it is characteristic of man's nature to perceive only one thing at once, that will most affect it which represents only one object at one time; and as, in a series of successive sensations, each possesses a certain degree which is produced by all the preceding sensations, and acts upon all those which follow it, that series will have the greatest effect in which the single parts consist together in a perfectly similar relation. Now all this is true of music. The exact sequence of time, moreover, is its peculiar and essential property; this is all that is decided in it. The series which it presents but feebly impels us to any definite sensation. It gives us a theme, to which we can supply infinite texts; and that which the hearer really interweaves with this basis, in so far as he is, in general, congenially disposed, springs up freely and naturally from the very fulness of his soul; and the latter more readily and eagerly embraces it than anything else that is actually supplied or intruded on our sensations, which often engrosses us more from its being perceived rather than felt. As it does not belong to me to examine the nature and properties of music, I will not stay to observe its other striking characteristics, such as that it evokes tones from natural objects, and therein keeps closer to nature than painting, sculpture, or poetry. I only wished, in introducing it, to illustrate more clearly the different character of sensuous impressions.

But the manner of influence just described, is not peculiar to music alone. Kant* observes it to be possible with a union of shifting colours, and it characterizes still more

* Kritik der Urtheilskraft, p. 211 ff.

remarkably the impressions we receive from the sense of touch. Even in taste it is unmistakable. In taste, also, there are different gradations of satisfaction, which, as it were, long to be resolved, and disappear, after the solution, in a series of diminishing vibrations. This influence may be least noticeable, perhaps, in the sense of smell. Now, as in the sensitive man it is the progress of sensation, its degree, its ranging increase and decrease, its pure and perfect harmony, which chiefly engage us, and indeed are more really attractive than the substance itself (forgetting, as we do, that the nature of the substance mainly determines the degree, and still more, the harmony of the progression); and further, as the sensitive man, like the image of spring teeming with blossoms, is the spectacle which is above all others the most fascinating; so also, in the fine arts, it is this image of his sensations which man especially strives to discover. And thus it is that painting and sculpture appropriate it to themselves. The eye of Guido Reni's Madonna is not confined in its expression to the limits of a single, fleeting glance. The tense and straining muscles of the Borghisian Gladiator foretell the blow he is about to deal. In a still higher degree does poetry employ this image. And, to make my idea clearer, without wishing to direct especial attention to the comparative excellence of the fine arts, I would observe that they exercise their influence in two ways, and while these are shared by each, we find them combined in very different manner. They immediately convey ideas, or they excite sensations, thus attuning the soul to an internal harmony, and enriching and exalting its powers. Now, in proportion as one of these sources of influence borrows aid from the other, it weakens the force of its own peculiar impression. Poetry unites both in the highest degree, and it is therefore, in this respect, the most perfect of all the fine arts; but when we regard it in another light, it is also the most weak and imperfect. While it represents its objects less vividly than painting and sculpture, it does not address itself so impressively to sensation as song and music. But, not to speak of that many-sidedness which so especially characterizes poetry, we are ready to overlook this imperfection when we perceive that it is nearest to the true internal nature of man, since it clothes not only thought, but sensation, with the most delicate veil.

But to continue, the energizing sensuous impressions (for I only refer to the arts by way of illustrating these) act in different ways; this is partly owing to the fact that their progression is more rhythmically proportional, and partly that the elements of the impressions themselves, or their substance, as it were, more violently affects the soul. Thus it is that the human voice, of equal melodiousness and quality, affects us more powerfully than a lifeless instrument. For nothing is ever so near to us as the personal, physical feeling; and where this feeling is itself called into play, the effect produced is the greatest. But here, as always, the disproportionate power of the substance suppresses, as it were, the delicacy of the form; and there must always exist a just relation between these. Wherever there is such a misproportion,, the proper equilibrium can be restored by increasing the power of the weaker, or diminishing that of the stronger element. But it is always wrong to effect anything by weakening or diminution, unless the power reduced be not natural, but artificial; only when this is the case should any limitation be imposed. It is better that it should destroy itself than slowly die away. But I may not dwell longer on this subject. I hope to have sufficiently elucidated my idea, although I would fain avow the embarrassment under which I necessarily labour in this inquiry; for, as the interesting nature of the subject, and the impossibility of borrowing from other writers just those results which were necessary (as I know of none who proceed exactly from the same point of view), invited me, on the one hand, to expatiate at somewhat greater length ; on the other, the reflection that these considerations do not strictly belong to this subject, but are only subordinate lemmas, served to recall me within my appropriate limits. I have only to request that such a difficulty be not forgotten, in regard to my subsequent observations.

Although it is impossible to abstract the subject completely, I have endeavoured hitherto to confine my remarks to sensuous impressions only as such. But the sensual and spiritual are linked together by a mysterious bond, of which our hearts are distinctly conscious, though it remains hidden from our eyes. To this double nature of the visible and invisible world—to the deep-implanted longing for the latter, coupled with the feeling of the sweet necessity of the former, we owe all sound and logical systems of philosophy, truly based on the immutable principles of our nature, just as to the same source we are able to trace the most visionary and incoherent reveries. A constant endeavour to unite these two elements, so that each may rob as little as possible from the other, has always seemed to me the true end of wisdom. This æsthetic feeling, in virtue of which the sensuous is to us a veil of the spiritual, and the spiritual the living principle of the world of sense, is everywhere unmistakable. The continual contemplation of this "physiognomy" of nature forms the true man. For nothing exercises such a vast influence on the whole character, as the expression of the spiritual in the sensuous,—of the sublime, the simple, the beautiful in all the works of nature and products of art which surround us. Here, too, we find the difference manifested between the energizing and other sensuous impressions. If the ultimate object of all our mortal striving is solely to discover, nourish, and re-create what truly exists in ourselves and others, although in its original for ever invisible,—if it is the intuitive anticipation of this which so endears and consecrates each of its symbols in our eyes, then the nearer do we approach to this original essence in contemplating the image of its restlessly-impellent energy. We commune with it in a language which is indeed difficult, and often misinterpreted, but which often startles us with the surest gleams and premonitions of truth, whilst the form and image of that energy are still more remote from that truth which we thus guess at.

This is the peculiar soil, moreover, on which the beautiful springs up and flourishes, and still more especially the sublime, which brings us yet nearer to Deity. The necessity for some purer satisfaction, far removed in its objects from all preconceived design and without conception, points out to man his descent from the invisible; and the feeling of his utter inadequateness to the surpassing fulness of the object, blends together, in a union at once the most human and divine, infinite greatness with the most devoted humility. Were it not for his feeling for the beautiful, man would cease to love things for their own sake; were it not for the sublime, he would lose that sense of dutiful submission which disdains every recompense, and ignores unworthy fear. The study of the beautiful bestows taste; that of the sublime (if it also may be studied, and the feeling and representation of it is not the fruit of genius) brings justly-balanced greatness. But taste alone, which must always repose on greatness as its basis (since it is only the great which requires measure, and only the powerful, composure), blends all the tones of a perfectly-adjusted being into exquisite harmony. It induces in all our impressions, even those which are purely spiritual, something so concordant, so composed, so concentrated into one focal point. Where taste is wanting, sensual desire is rude and unrestrained; and although without it, scientific inquiries may be both acute and profound, there is no refinement, no polish, nothing fruitful in their application. In general, where there is no taste, the greatest depth of thought and the noblest treasures of wisdom are barren and lifeless, and even the sublime strength of the moral will is shorn of all its graceful and genial blessing.

To inquire and to create;—these are the grand centres around which all human pursuits revolve, or at least to these objects do they all more or less directly refer. Before inquiry can fathom the very essence of things, or penetrate to the limits of reason, it presupposes, in addition to profundity, a rich diversity and genial warmth of soul—the harmonious exertion of all the human faculties combined. It is the analytical philosopher alone, perhaps, who is able to arrive at his results through the calm, but cold processes of reason. But real depth of thought and a mind which has found means to cultivate all its powers to an equal degree of perfection, are essentially necessary to discover the link which unites *synthetical* principles. Thus Kant, who, it may be truly said, was never surpassed in profoundness, will often be charged with a kind of dreamy enthusiasm when treating of morals or æsthetics, and has indeed been so accused; but while I am willing to confess that there are passages (as, for example, his interpretation of the prismatic colours*) which, though rare, appear to indicate something of this nature, I am only led to deplore my own want of intellectual depth. To follow these ideas out, would naturally lead us to that difficult but interesting inquiry into the

* 2nd Edit. (Berlin, 1793) p. 172. Kant calls the modifications of light in colour a language which nature addresses to us, and which seems to have some deeper significance. "Thus the spotless whiteness of the lily seems to dispose the heart to ideas of innocence, and the other colours in their order from red to violet:—1. To the idea of sublimity; 2. Of courage; 3. Of sincerity; 4. Of kindliness; 5. Of humility; 6. Of firmness; 7. Of tenderness."

essential difference between the metaphysician and the poet. And if a thorough re-investigation of this were not to reverse, perhaps, my previous conclusions, I would limit my definition of the difference to this, that the philosopher concerns himself with perceptions alone, and the poet, on the contrary, with sensations; while both require the same measure and cultivation of mental power. But to establish this would lead me too far astray from my immediate subject, and I trust to have shown already, by my previous arguments, that, even to form the calmest thinker, the pleasures of sense and fancy must have often played around the soul. But to pass from transcendental to psychological inquiries (where man as he appears is the object of our studies), would not *he* explore most deeply the genus which is richest in forms, and represent it most truly and vividly, to whose own sensations the fewest of these forms are strange?

Hence it is that the man who is thus developed displays the full beauty of his character when he enters into practical life—when, externally and internally, he enriches with a thousand new creations that which he has received. The analogy between the laws of plastic nature and those of intellectual creation, has been already noticed by a mind* of singular power of penetration, and established by striking proofs. But perhaps his exposition would have been still more interesting, and psychology enriched with the results of a more extended knowledge, if, instead of inquiring into the inscrutable development of the germ, the process of intellectual creation had been shown to be, as it were, the more exquisite flower and ethereal beauty of the corporeal.

To extend our remarks :—with respect to the moral life, to that which seems to be the especial province of cold, abstract reason, we would observe that the idea of the sublime alone enables us to obey absolute and unconditional

* F. v. Dalberg : vom Bilden und Erfinden.

laws, at once humanly, through the medium of feeling, and divinely and disinterestedly, through the utter absence of all ulterior reference to happiness or misfortune. The feeling of the insufficiency of human strength to the full performance of the moral law, the profound consciousness that the most virtuous is he only who feels most inly how unattainably high the law is exalted above him, tend to inspire awe—a sensation which seems to be no more shrouded in a corporeal veil than is necessary not to dazzle our eyes by the full and immediate splendour. Now, when the moral law obliges us to regard every man as an end to himself, it becomes blended with that feeling for the beautiful which loves to animate the merest clay, that even in it, it may rejoice in an individual existence, and which receives and enfolds man all the more completely and lovingly in that it is independent of conception, and is not therefore limited to the few characteristics, which, though separate and single, are yet all that conception can embrace.

The union with the feeling for the beautiful seems as if it would impair the purity of the moral will, and it might, and indeed would, have this effect, if this feeling itself were to become the sole motive to morality. But it will only claim the duty of discovering those more varied applications of the moral law which would otherwise escape the cold, and hence in such cases, ruder processes of reason; and since we are not forbidden to receive happiness in such intimate union with virtue, but only to barter virtue for this happiness, it will also enjoy the privilege of bestowing on human nature its sweetest and dearest feelings. In general, the more I reflect on this subject, the less does this difference to which I refer appear to be either subtle or fanciful. However eagerly man may strive to grasp at enjoyment—however he may try to represent to himself a constant union subsisting between happiness and virtue, even under the most unfavourable circumstances, his soul still remains alive to the grandeur of the moral law.   He cannot screen himself from the influence and authority of this imposing grandeur over his actions, and it is only from being penetrated with a sense of it, that he acts without reference to enjoyment; for he never loses the consciousness that no misfortune whatever would compel him to adopt another behaviour.

It is, however, true that the soul only acquires this strength in a way similar to that we before described—only by a mighty internal pressure, and a manifold external struggle.   But strength properly branches out, like its substance, from man's sensuous nature; and however seemingly remote, still reposes on that as its central stem.   Now he who ceaselessly strives to exalt his faculties, and to infuse into them new youth and vigour by frequent enjoyment; who often calls in his strength of character to aid him in asserting his independence of sensualism, while he endeavours to combine this independence with the most exquisite susceptibility; whose deep unerring sense unweariedly searches after the truth; whose just and delicate feeling for the beautiful leaves no attractive form unnoticed; whose impulse to receive into himself his external perceptions, and to impregnate them with new issues—to transform all shapes of beauty into his own individuality, and fuse into each his entire being,—strives to generate new forms of beauty;—such a one may cherish the consoling consciousness that he is in the true path to approach that ideal which even the boldest flight of fancy has ventured to point out to human aspirations.

I have in this brief sketch endeavoured to show how intimately sensualism, with all its beneficial consequences, is interwoven with the whole tissue of human life and pursuits.   Although such a topic is in itself somewhat foreign to a political essay, it was appropriate and even necessary in the order of ideas adopted in this inquiry; and in these remarks on sensualism, I designed to advocate the justice of extending an ampler degree of freedom towards its manifestations, and of regarding its important influences with greater respect. Still, I would not blind myself to the fact that sensualism is also the immediate source of innumerable physical and moral evils. Even morally speaking, it is only beneficial in its operation when it subsists in a just relationship with the exercise of the mental faculties; it acquires a hurtful preponderance with a dangerous facility. When once the equilibrium is destroyed, human pleasure becomes degraded to mere animal gratification, and taste disappears, or becomes distorted into unnatural directions. At the same time, I would make the reservation with regard to this last expression, and chiefly with reference to certain one-sided opinions, that we are not to condemn anything as *unnatural* which does not exactly fulfil this or that purpose of nature, but only whatever frustrates its general ultimate design with regard to man. Now this is, that his nature should always be developing itself to higher degrees of perfection, and hence, especially, that his thinking and susceptive powers should always be indissolubly united in just and proportionate degrees of strength. But again, a misrelation may arise between the process and order in which a man developes and manifests his powers, and the means of action and enjoyment afforded by his peculiar position; and this misrelation is a fresh source of evil. Now, according to our former principles, the State may not attempt to act upon the citizen's peculiar condition with any reference to *positive* ends. Under such a *negative policy*, therefore, this condition of the citizen would not acquire so definite and constrained a form, and its greater freedom (coupled with the fact that it would be chiefly influenced and directed in

that freedom by the citizen's own ways of thinking and acting) would already operate to lessen and remove that misrelation. Still, the fact that, even under such a supposition,
the original danger would remain—a danger which is far
from being unimportant or imaginary—might suggest the
necessity of checking and opposing the corruption of morals
by laws and State institutions.

But even granting that such laws and institutions were
effectual, their hurtfulness would keep pace with their activity. A State, in which the citizens were compelled or ac-
tuated by such means to obey even the best of laws, might
be a tranquil, peaceable, prosperous State; but it would
always seem to me a multitude of well cared-for slaves,
rather than a nation of free and independent men, with no
restraint save such as was required to prevent any infringements on right. There are, doubtless, many methods of
producing given actions and sentiments only; but none
of these lead to true moral perfection. Sensual impulses,
urging to the commission of certain actions, or the continuing necessity of refraining from these, gradually come to en-
gender a habit; through the force of habit the satisfaction
which was at first connected with these impulses alone, is
transferred to the action itself; the inclination, which at
first only slumbered under the pressure of necessity, becomes wholly stifled; and thus man may be led to keep his
actions within the limits of virtue, and to a certain extent
to entertain virtuous sentiments. But neither is his spiritual energy exalted by such a process, nor his views of his
destination and his own worth made clearer, nor does his
will gain greater power to conquer the dictates of his rebel-
lious desires; and hence, he does not advance a single step
towards true, actual perfection. They, therefore, who would
pursue the task of developing man without any reference
to external ends will never make use of such inadequate

means. For, setting aside the fact that coercion and guidance can never succeed in producing virtue, they manifestly tend to weaken power; and what are tranquil order and outward morality without true moral strength and virtue? Moreover, however great an evil immorality may be, we must not forget that it is not without its beneficial consequences. It is only through extremes that men can arrive at the middle path of wisdom and virtue. Extremes, like large masses shining afar off, must operate at a distance. In order that blood be supplied to the most delicate ramifications of the arteries, there must be copious sources in the larger vessels. To wish to disturb the order of nature in these respects, is to acquiesce in a moral, in order to prevent a physical evil.

Moreover, I think we err in supposing that the danger of immorality is either so great or so urgent; and while much that I have said tends more or less to establish this, the following conclusions may serve to give it additional confirmation :—

1. Man is naturally more disposed to beneficent than selfish actions. This we learn even from the history of savages. The domestic virtues have something in them so inviting and genial, and the public virtues of the citizen something so grand and inspiring, that even he who is barely uncorrupted, is seldom able to resist their charm.

2. Freedom exalts power; and, as is always the collateral effect of increasing strength, tends to induce a spirit of liberality. Coercion stifles power, and engenders all selfish desires, and all the mean artifices of weakness. Coercion may prevent many transgressions; but it robs even actions which are legal of a portion of their beauty. Freedom may lead to many transgressions, but it lends even to vices a less ignoble form.

3. The man who is abandoned to himself arrives with

greater difficulty at just principles; but they manifest themselves ineffaceably in his actions. He who is designedly
guided, receives such principles with greater facility; but
still they give way before his energies, however much enfeebled.

4. All political arrangements, in that they have to bring
a variety of widely-discordant interests into unity and harmony, necessarily occasion manifold collisions. From these
collisions spring misproportions between men's desires
and their powers; and from these, transgressions. The
more active the State is, the greater is the number of these.
If it were possible to make an accurate calculation of the
evils which police regulations occasion, and of those which
they prevent, the number of the former would, in all cases,
exceed that of the latter.

5. How far the strictest search into crimes actually committed, the infliction of just, well-measured, but irremissible
punishment, and the consequent rareness of moral impunity,
are really practicable, has never yet been duly tried.

I have now sufficiently shown, according to my views,
how questionable is every effort of the State to oppose or
even to prevent any dissoluteness of morals (in so far as it
does not imply injury to individual rights); how few are
the beneficial results to be expected from such attempts, as
regards morality; and how the exercise of such an influence
on the character of a nation, is not even necessary for the
preservation of security.

If now, in addition to this, we bring forward the principles
before unfolded, which disapprove of all State agency directed to *positive* aims, and which apply here with especial
force, since it is precisely the moral man who feels every
restriction most deeply; reflecting, further, that if there is
one aspect of development more than any other which owes
its highest beauty to freedom, this is precisely the culture

of character and morals; then the justice of the following principle will be sufficiently manifest, viz. *that the State must wholly refrain from every attempt to operate directly or indirectly on the morals and character of the nation, otherwise than as such a policy may become inevitable as a natural consequence of its other absolutely necessary measures; and that everything calculated to promote such a design, and particularly all special supervision of education, religion, sumptuary laws, etc., lies wholly outside the limits of its legitimate activity.*

# CHAPTER IX.

THE SOLICITUDE OF THE STATE FOR SECURITY MORE
ACCURATELY AND POSITIVELY DEFINED.—FURTHER DE-
VELOPMENT OF THE IDEA OF SECURITY.

AFTER having now completed the more important and difficult portions of the present inquiry, and approached nearer
to the solution of the great problem which it involves, it
becomes necessary to review its progress up to this point,
and endeavour to sum up its results.

Firstly, then, we have seen sufficient reasons for withdrawing the exercise of State solicitude from all such objects as do not immediately relate to the external or internal
security of its citizens. In the second place, this same security has been represented as the real object of political
activity; and, lastly, it has been agreed, that no efforts are
allowable for the promotion of this object which are designed to operate on the morals and character of the nation
itself, or to impart or counteract in them any definite direction. To a certain extent, therefore, the question as to the
proper limits of State agency appears to be already fully
solved, seeing that the sphere of this agency is confined to
the preservation of security; and as to the means available
for that purpose, still more narrowly restricted to those
which do not interfere, for State ends, with the development
of national character, or, rather, do not mould and fashion
it with a view to those ends. For although, it is true, this
definition is so far purely negative, yet that which remains
after this abstraction of different departments of solicitude

is of itself sufficiently distinct. That is, it is evident that political activity can only extend its influence to such actions as imply a direct trespass on the rights of others; to the task of deciding in cases of disputed right; to redressing the wronged, and punishing the wrong-doers. But the idea of security,—towards defining which nothing further has been observed than that it embraces security against the attacks of foreign enemies, and against the aggressive spirit of fellow-citizens,—is too wide and comprehensive not to require some more special exposition. For, just as there are great and important differences between the modifications brought about by that advice which only seeks to persuade, and those consequent on importunate recommendation, and between these and the influence of positive coercion; and just as the degrees of unfairness and injustice may vary, from actions exercised within the limits of one's own right, but possibly hurtful to another, to those which likewise do not trespass those limits, but often or always tend to disturb some other in the enjoyment of his own, and again from these to actual encroachments on another's rightful property; just in like manner does the idea of security vary in extent and application, since we may understand it of security against some particular kind or degree of coercive influence, or against some certain extent of wrong. Now this very interpretation of the term security is of extreme importance; and if it is received in a too vague or, on the other hand, too narrow and restricted sense, all lines and limits are confused; while, without some distinct definition, it is impossible to re-adjust those limits and repair that confusion.

Again, the active means to be entrusted to the State for the promotion of its ends, once determined, constitute the subject of a still more accurate and minute investigation. For, although we have disapproved of any attempt on the part of the State, directed to the reformation of morals, there still remains, in this respect, too large and indefinite a field for political enterprise. There has been but little decided, for example, as to the bearing of restrictive enactments on those actions which immediately violate the rights of others; and as to how far the State may proceed in preventing actual crimes by stopping up their sources, not in the character of the citizens, but in the opportunities which facilitate their commission. Now, how far and dangerously it is possible to err in this respect, is already shown by the fact that the very solicitude for freedom has disposed more than one of singular judgment and penetration, to make the State responsible for the whole welfare of its citizens; believing that such a comprehensive arrangement would serve to promote all free and spontaneous activity. I am therefore ready to confess, in view of these considerations, that I have as yet done nothing but separate such large tracts as lie clearly without the circle of political activity, and have not yet endeavoured to draw its precise demarcations; more especially wherever its limits were questionable or unsettled.

This therefore still remains to be done; and, even though I may not be wholly successful in the attempt, it yet seems well for me to ascertain the reasons for the failure, and represent the difficulties incident to the inquiry as clearly and fully as possible. And, in any case, I hope to conclude the subject in a short compass, as all the principles I require for the task have been already discussed and settled, as far as my abilities would allow.

I call the citizens of a State *secure*, when, living together in the full enjoyment of their due rights of person and property, they are out of the reach of any external disturbance from the encroachments of others; and hence I would call *security* (if the expression does not seem too brief for distinctness) the *assurance of legal freedom*. Now this security is not of necessity disturbed by all such actions as impede a man in the free exercise of his powers, and in the full enjoyment of all that belongs to him, but only by those which do this *unrightfully*. This sense which we assign to the word, and the definition just adapted to express it, are not to be supposed arbitrarily chosen and appended. Both follow immediately from our previous conclusions; and it is only with this sense of the term security, that our former reasoning can find application. For it is only actual violations of right which require any other power to counteract them than that which every individual himself possesses; it is the prevention of such violations alone which is pure gain to true development, while every other manifestation of political enterprise throws nought but obstacles in its way; and, lastly, it is this State-duty alone which has its source in the infallible precepts of absolute necessity, while every other is based on the shifting ground of a utility, estimated according to weak and treacherous probabilities.

Those whose security is to be preserved are, on the one hand, all the citizens, in perfect legal equality, and, on the other, the State itself. The extent of this latter object, or the security of the State, is determined by the extent of the rights assigned to it, and through these by the nature and extent of its aims. As I have hitherto argued, it may not demand security for anything save the power entrusted to its hands, and the resources allotted to its disposal. Further, it should not, with a view to this security, restrict the citizen when, without violating any actual right (and hence, with the understanding that he is not bound to the State by any personal or temporary relation, as, for instance, in time of war), he would withdraw himself or his property from the political community. For the State organism is merely a subordinate means, to which man, the true end, is not to be sacrificed; unless such a collision should occur as that in which the individual would not be bound to surrender himself, and yet the community would possess the right of taking him as a sacrifice. Moreover, according to our former principles, the State is denied all positive solicitude for the citizen's welfare; and nothing can be necessary in order to preserve security which tends precisely to repress freedom, and along with it this very security itself.

Disturbances of security are occasioned either by actions which violate in themselves the rights of others, or by those which only imply the apprehension of this in their consequences. Now, both these kinds of action (with certain modifications which will shortly occupy our attention) are to be prohibited by the State, and, as far as this can be done, prevented; when once they are committed, it must try to render them, as far as possible, innoxious, by extending legal redress for the wrong sustained, and by punishment, to lessen the frequency of such actions in future. From the necessity for these duties (to adhere to the terms usually employed), come police, civil and criminal laws. In addition to these, however, there comes another object under the general head of solicitude for security; and, on account of its peculiar nature, it requires a wholly distinct treatment. There is a class of citizens to whom the principles we have unfolded (since they presuppose men to be in the enjoyment of their natural faculties) can only be accommodated with considerable modifications. I allude to those who have not yet arrived at the age of maturity, or who, through idiocy or mania, have not the use of their proper human powers. It is evident that the State must provide as well for the security of such persons; and as we can easily foresee, their peculiar position must require a special policy to be adopted towards them. We must therefore, in the last place, consider the relation in which the State stands to all infants among its citizens, in character (to use the familiar expression) of their chief guardian.

Having before sufficiently treated of security against foreign enemies, I believe I have now succeeded in marking out all the objects towards which the State is to direct its active solicitude. Far from pretending to penetrate at all profoundly into all the great and difficult subjects I have enumerated, I shall be content to develope the fundamental principles in each, as briefly as possible, and as far as comes within the scope of my present design. It is only when this has been done that we can regard our endeavour as complete —that we can suppose ourselves to have attempted to exhaust the proposed question in all its important bearings, and to trace on all sides the proper boundary-lines of political activity.

# CHAPTER X.

ON THE SOLICITUDE OF THE STATE FOR SECURITY WITH RESPECT TO ACTIONS WHICH DIRECTLY RELATE TO THE AGENT ONLY. (POLICE LAWS.)

WE now come to accompany man throughout all the complex and manifold relations which his life in society presents, and shall begin with considering the simplest of these, or that in which (although in union with others) man remains strictly within the limits of what pertains to himself, and engages in nothing that refers immediately to the rights of others. It is to this aspect of the civil relations that the greater number of our so-called police, or preventive, laws are directed; since, however indefinite this expression may be, it still conveys to us the general and important idea, that such laws relate to the means of averting violations of the rights of others, while they have nothing to do with the violations of such right which are actually committed. Now they either operate to restrict actions whose immediate consequences are calculated to endanger the rights of others; or they impose limitations on those which usually end in transgressions of law; or, lastly, they may design to determine what is necessary for the preservation or efficient exercise of the political power itself. I must here overlook the fact that those regulations which do not relate to security, but are directed to the positive welfare of the citizen, are most commonly classed under this head; since it does not fall in with the system of division I have adopted. Now, according to the principles we have already determined, the State ought not to interfere with this, the simplest of human relations, except where there are just grounds for apprehending some violation of its own rights, or those of its citizens. And as to the rights of the State, it should here be borne in mind that such rights are granted only for the sake of protecting security. In no case, then, should prohibitive laws be enacted, when the advantage or disadvantage refers solely to the proprietor. Again, it is not enough to justify such restrictions, that an action should imply damage to another person; it must, at the same time, encroach upon his rights. But this second position requires explanation. Right, then, is never infringed on but when some one is deprived of a portion of what properly belongs to him, or of his personal freedom, without, or against, his will. But when, on the contrary, there occurs no such deprivation,—when one individual does not overstep the boundary of another's right, then, whatever disadvantage may accrue to the latter, there is no diminution of privilege. Neither is there any such diminution when the injury itself does not follow until he who sustains it also becomes active on his side, and, as it were, takes up the action, or, at least, does not oppose it as far as he can.

The application of these definitions is sufficiently evident, and I will only pause to mention one or two remarkable examples. According to these principles then it will be seen, that we cannot conceive the injustice of any actions which only create offence, and especially as regards religion and morals. He who utters or performs anything calculated to wound the conscience and moral sense of others, may indeed act immorally; but, so long as he is not chargeable with obtrusiveness in these respects, he violates no right. The others are free to cut off all intercourse with such a person, and, should circumstances render this impossible, they must submit to the unavoidable inconvenience of associating with men of uncongenial character; not forget-

G

ting, moreover, that the obnoxious party may likewise be annoyed by the display of peculiar traits in them.   Even a possible exposure to more positively hurtful influences,—as where the beholding this or that action, or the listening to a particular argument, was calculated to impair the virtue, or mislead the reason and sound sense of others,—would not be sufficient to justify restrictions on freedom.   Whoever spoke or acted thus did not therein infringe directly on the right of any other; and it was free to those who were exposed to the influence of such words and actions to counteract the evil impression on themselves with the strength of will and the principles of reason.   Hence, then, however great the evils that may follow from overt immorality and seductive errors of reasoning, there still remains this excellent consequence, that in the former case the strength and resistive force of character, in the latter the spirit of toleration and diversity of view, are brought to the test, and reap benefit in the process.   It is scarcely necessary to mention that in the instance I have just taken, I have confined my view to its influence on the security of the citizens.   For I have already endeavoured to exhibit the relation of such actions to national morality, and to show what may or may not be allowed to the State with regard to them, on that ground.

Since, however, there are many things of which the correct decision requires a wholly special knowledge, and since, in regard to these, security might be disturbed if any one should unthinkingly or designedly turn the ignorance of others to his own advantage, the citizen should have the option, in such cases, of applying to the State for counsel. The most striking instances of what I mean,—whether we consider the frequent necessity for such special knowledge, the difficulty attending just discrimination, or, lastly, the magnitude of the injury to be apprehended,—are furnished by those cases in which the professional services of physicians and advocates are put in requisition. Now, in order to meet the wants and wishes of the nation in these respects, it is not only advisable but necessary that the State should examine into the qualifications of those who destine themselves for such pursuits, provided they agree to submit themselves to its tests; and, furnishing them with testimonials of fitness in case of a favourable issue of the inquiry, to acquaint the citizens that they can only confide with certainty in those who have thus been proved. Beyond this, however, the State may not proceed, or withhold from those who have declined or failed in examination the exercise of their avocation, and from the public the use of their services. Neither should it be allowed to extend such supervision to any other occupations than those which are not designed to act on the internal, but only on the external life of man, and in which he is not himself required to co-operate, but only to remain passive and obedient, and where the truth or falsity of results is the only thing of importance; or, secondly, such regulations are proper in those cases where due discrimination requires the knowledge of some wholly special department, and is not attainable by the mere exercise of reason and the practical ability of judging, and further where the rarity of their occurrence renders the very seeking of advice difficult. Should the State proceed further than is prescribed by this last limitation, it falls into the danger of rendering the nation indolent, inactive, and too much inclined to repose on the knowledge and judgment of others; while, on the other hand, the very want of positive assistance invites men rather to enrich their own knowledge and experience, and knits the citizens together by a thousand intimate relations, inasmuch as they are left more exclusively dependent on each other. Should the State fail to observe the first limitation we have pointed out, that it is not to withhold a man from the free exercise of his chosen pursuit because he has not submitted himself to its tests of capability, then, besides the evils just alluded to, all those hurtful consequences will naturally follow which we exposed in detail in the beginning of this essay. It is evident then—to choose another remarkable example illustrative of our present subject—that in the case of religious teachers State regulations cannot at all be applied. For as to what points of fitness should the State examine them? In the belief of some particular dogmas? We have already fully shown that religion is in no way dependent on these. Should it ground its estimate on the degree of intellectual power in general? In the teacher of religion, whose task it is to present things to his audience in an intimate connection with their individual life, almost the sole point of importance is the relation between his reason and theirs,—a consideration which already argues such an *à priori* decision to be impossible. Should it judge then of moral character and integrity? For these there is no other test than that which is least adapted to the political function, viz. inquiry into the previous conduct and circumstances of the candidates, etc. Lastly, regulations of this nature—even in the cases we have ourselves approved —should, in general, only be adopted when the will of the nation demands them. For, of themselves, they are not even necessary among free men, who are developed through the very circumstance of their freedom; and further, they might be constantly liable to serious abuse. As, in general, it is not my design to examine into single objects in detail, but rather to define the fundamental principles which embrace all these in their application, I shall once more briefly indicate the only point of view from which I contemplate such regulations. The State, then, is not to concern itself in any way with the positive welfare of its citizens, and hence, no more with their life or health, except where these are imperilled by the actions of others; but it is to keep a vigilant eye on their security, though only in so far as this might suffer from the attempts of the designing to turn the ignorance of others to their own advantage. Still, in such cases of deception as that to which we refer, the victim of the imposture must necessarily have been persuaded into conviction; and as in such relations the flux and reflux of different modifying influences from one party to the other precludes the application of any general rule, and as the very liability to imposition which freedom opens out tends to discipline men's prudence and foresight, I esteem it more accordant with fundamental principles (in a theory which is necessarily removed from practical application) to confine prohibitive laws to those cases only in which actions are done without the will of another, or still more, in direct opposition to it. The general tenour of my arguments will serve to indicate the consistent treatment of other cases, should these present themselves*.

While we have hitherto confined our attention only to the nature of those consequences, flowing from an action, which bring it under the operation of State supervision, we have yet to inquire whether the mere prospective possibility of such consequences is sufficient to justify the restriction of given actions, or whether this is only requisite where those consequences follow in the necessary course. Freedom may suffer if we adopt the former supposition; if the latter, security may be endangered. It is therefore sufficiently clear that a middle path should be pursued; but to give any general definition of this seems to me impossible.

* It might appear that the cases here mentioned do not so much belong to the present chapter as to the next, since they concern actions which refer immediately to others. But I have not here considered the case in which a physician actually treats a patient, or a lawyer really undertakes a suit; but only of the choice of a means of gaining a livelihood in these respects. I only propose the question whether the State should restrict such a choice; and this choice alone does not relate directly to any one.

It is certain that the deliberation in such cases must be guided at once by considerations of the extent of the injury, and of the restrictions on freedom implied in the given law. But the proper estimation of these does not admit, properly speaking, of any general rule; and all calculations of probability are eminently fallacious. Theory therefore can only point out these moments of deliberation. In the reference to practice, I am of opinion that special circumstances should be chiefly regarded, and not so much the general cases; and that only when observation of the past and considerations of the present combine to represent a restriction as indispensable, should it ever be resolved on. The right of nature, when applied to the social life of a number of men, defines the boundary lines unmistakably. It condemns all actions in which, with his own fault, one man encroaches on the due province of another, and hence, includes all those cases in which the injury strictly arises from a blamable oversight, or where it is always associated with the action, or with such a degree of probability in the consequence, that the agent either perceives it or at least becomes accountable by overlooking it. In all other cases the injury proceeds from chance, and of course the agent is not bound to repair its effects. Any wider application than this, could only be gained from the tacit agreement of those living together; and this is again something positive. But that the State should rest here seems justly questionable; especially when we consider the importance of the injury to be apprehended, and the possibility of rendering the restriction imposed on freedom, only moderately hurtful to the citizens. In such a case it is clear that the right is undeniable on the part of the State, since it is to provide for security, not only in so far as the enforcement of reparation is concerned where right has really been violated, but also in adopting means for preventing such wrongs. A third person, moreover, can only decide according to external characteristics. It is therefore impossible for the State to wait to see whether the citizens will fail in taking due precautions against dangerous actions, neither can it rely on the probability of their foreseeing the injury: where circumstances seem to represent the apprehension as urgent, it must rather restrict actions in themselves harmless.

In view of these considerations, therefore, we may be justified in laying down the following principle: *in order to provide for the security of its citizens, the State must prohibit or restrict such actions, referring immediately to the agents alone, as imply the infringement on others' rights in their consequences, or encroach in these on their freedom or property without or against their will; and further, it must forbid or restrict these actions when the probability of such consequences is fairly to be apprehended,—a probability in which it must necessarily consider the extent of the injury feared, and on the other hand the consequences of the restriction on freedom implied in the law contemplated. Beyond this, every limitation of personal freedom is to be condemned, as wholly foreign to the sphere of the State's activity.*

Since, according to the ideas I have unfolded, the protection of the rights of others affords the only just ground for these restrictions, the necessity for them must naturally disappear when this ground no longer exists; and hence when—for instance, in most police-regulations—the danger extends only to the circuit of the community, the village, the town, as soon as such a community expressly and unanimously demands that these restrictions should be abolished. The State must then relax its efforts, and content itself with punishing such injuries only as have occurred with an intentional or culpable violation of right.

For to put an end to strifes and dissensions among the
citizens is the only true interest of the State; and to the
promotion of this, the will of single citizens, even though
they are themselves the parties injured, should never be allowed to oppose obstacles.  If we suppose a community of
enlightened men,—fully instructed in their truest interests,
and therefore mutually well-disposed and closely united together,—we can easily imagine how voluntary contracts with
a view to their security, would be entered into among them;
contracts, for example, that this or that dangerous occupation
or manufacture should be carried on only in certain places
and at certain times, or even should be wholly prohibited.
Agreements of this kind are infinitely to be preferred to
any State arrangements.  For as it is the very persons who
enter into such contracts who are most conscious of their
necessity, and feel directly the advantage or disadvantage
accruing from them, it is clear that they will not be easily
formed without an evident want of such agreements ; that
they will be far more rigidly observed, being voluntarily
made ; that however considerable the restrictions they entail,
they will have a less hurtful influence on the character,
being the results of spontaneous activity ; and that, lastly,
springing as they would from a certain spirit of benevolence
and enlightenment, would still further contribute in their
turn to increase and diffuse both.  The best efforts of the
State should therefore aim at bringing men into such a condition by means of freedom, that associations would arise
with greater facility, and so supply the place of political
regulations in these and manifold similar instances.

I have not made any mention here of such laws as impose positive duties on the citizens, or the sacrifice or performance of anything either for the State or for each other,
though there are such laws everywhere among us. But, apart
from that application of his powers which every citizen,

where it is necessary, owes to the State (concerning which I shall have to speak hereafter), I do not esteem it good that the State should compel any one to do anything to gratify the wish or further the interests of another, even though he should receive the amplest compensation. For as everything and every pursuit, from the infinite diversity of human dispositions and desires, confers on each such various and inestimable benefits, and as these benefits may likewise vary infinitely in interest, importance, and necessity, the decision as to which good of the one, and which of the other, should be chosen as equivalent (though its difficulty should not deter us from it), is always attended with something harsh, and seems like passing sentence on the feelings and individuality of another. For this reason, moreover, that we cannot make any exact substitution except where the things in question are exactly of the same kind, real compensation is often utterly impossible, and can scarcely even be determined by a general rule.

In addition to these injurious consequences of the best of laws of this kind, there is always, moreover, an implied facility of possible abuse.

Further, the consideration of security (which alone rightly prescribes the sphere of State agency) does not render such regulations generally necessary, since every case in which this necessity occurs must be strictly exceptional: men, moreover, become more kindly disposed towards each other, and more prompt to render mutual assistance, the less they feel their self-love and sense of freedom to be wounded by an actual right of coercion on the part of others; and even though the mere humour and wholly groundless obstinacy of a man may happen to thwart an excellent undertaking, such an event is not sufficient to require that the power of the State should be thrown into the contest. In the physical world, it does not shatter every rock to pieces that juts out on the path of the wanderer. Obstacles serve to stimulate energy, and discipline forethought; none uselessly obstruct, save those which arise from human injustice; but that obstinacy is not such an impediment which may indeed be bent by the force of laws in single cases, but can only be removed by the blessed influences of freedom. These reasons, of which a brief summary is all that can be given here, seem yet sufficient to make us yield to iron necessity alone; and the State should content itself with securing to men their natural right to sacrifice the freedom and property of another in order to avert their own ruin.

Lastly, there are many police laws framed to meet actions which are performed, it is true, within the limits of the agent's right, but that not his exclusively, it being shared in conjunction with others. In such cases, restrictions on freedom are evidently far less questionable; as in property that is common, every joint proprietor has the right of gainsay. Such common property we have, for instance, in roads, in rivers flowing through different properties, in squares and streets of towns.

# CHAPTER XI.

ON THE SOLICITUDE OF THE STATE FOR SECURITY WITH
RESPECT TO SUCH OF THE CITIZENS' ACTIONS AS RE-
LATE DIRECTLY TO OTHERS. (CIVIL LAWS.)

THE subject to which we have now to direct our attention,
or the consideration of actions which relate immediately to
others, although it is in general more complicated than the
last, does not imply so much difficulty as regards the present inquiry. For where rights are infringed on by such
actions, it is clearly the duty of the State to restrict them,
and compel the agents to repair the injury they have inflicted. But according to the position we endeavoured to enforce in a preceding chapter, these actions do no violence to
right except when they deprive another of a part of his
freedom or possessions without, or against, his will. When
any one has suffered wrong, he has a right to redress; but
when once, as a member of a community, he has transferred his private revenge to the State, to nothing more.
He, therefore, who has committed the wrong is bound to
restore to him who has sustained it, all of which he has
been deprived; or, should this be impossible, to make sufficient amends, standing security for this to the full extent
of his means and of all that his powers may enable him to
acquire. To deprive a man of his personal liberty,—as is
practised, for instance, in the case of insolvent debtors,—can
only be admitted as a subordinate means, where otherwise
the creditor should run the risk of losing the debtor's future
earnings. Now while the State is not to refuse any just

means of redress to the person injured, it must take care that a spirit of revenge does not turn this fair demand into a pretext for injustice. This seems the more necessary when we reflect, first, that in a state of nature the person originally committing the wrong would resist him who sought satisfaction, should he trespass the confines of right in his eagerness for revenge; whereas here, the irresistible authority of the State comes in to check further retaliation; and secondly, that general definitions (which are always necessary when a third is to decide) invariably tend to encourage the pretext before-mentioned. The imprisonment of debtors therefore might seem to require still further exceptions, as the greater number of laws relating to them allow.

Actions which are undertaken by mutual agreement are exactly similar to those which a man performs of himself, without immediate reference to others, and I have only to repeat of them what I have already observed of the latter. There is one class of such actions, however, which requires wholly special regulations; I mean those which are not concluded at once, but extend in their operation to the future. Under this head come promises or engagements which impose perfect duties on the parties to the engagement, whether it be mutual or not. By these, portions of property are made over from one person to another; and if the party transferring it retracts from his engagement by trying to recover what has been transferred, security is disturbed. It is therefore one of the most important duties pertaining to the State to see that such engagements are binding. But the restraint which every engagement imposes is then only just and salutary, when, firstly, the implied limitation extends to him alone who enters into it; and secondly, when he has in general, and at the time of the engagement, acted with a proper capacity of reflection, and exercised a free power of decision. Wherever such is not the case, coercion is as unjust in principle as it is pernicious in its effects. On the one hand, also, the deliberation as regards the future can never be perfectly just and complete; and on the other, there are many obligations contracted, of a nature to impose such fetters on liberty, as prove serious hindrances to the man's complete development. Hence there devolves a second duty on the State— to refuse the support of the law to such engagements as are contrary to right, and to take all necessary precautions (consistent with the security of property) to prevent a moment's want of reflection from entailing such restrictions on a man as to retard or prevent his own perfect development. It comes within the province of juridical theories, to detail all that is necessary for the validity of contracts or engagements. It only remains for me to observe, with regard to their objects, that a State, to which (according to our former principles) nothing beyond the solicitude for security is allowed, may not regard any other objects as exceptional save those which are already shown to be such by general considerations of right, or by the solicitude for security. Of this class we may notice the following cases, as being the most remarkable :—1. When the party promising cannot transfer any right of coercion without making himself a tool for the designs of others—as, for example, in every contract which ends in the slavery of the person contracting; 2. Where the party promising has no power to grant what is promised, according to its very nature—as is the case, for instance, in all matters of feeling or belief; 3. When the promise in itself, or in its implied consequences, is either incompatible with, or dangerous to, the rights of others, in which case the principles established in our last chapter are here also strictly applicable. Now the difference between these cases is this, that in the first and second the State must only refuse the right of coercion provided by its laws, without preventing the formation or execution of such engagements, in so far as this execution is mutual; while, in the last instance we have mentioned, it not only can, but must, forbid the very act of engagement itself.

Still, even where there is nothing to be objected to the validity of a contract, the State should have the power of lessening the restrictions which men impose on one another, even with their own consent, and (by facilitating the release from such engagements) of preventing a moment's decision from hindering their freedom of action for too long a period of life. When, however, a mere transfer of things is implied in the contract, without any other personal relation, I do not consider such a course to be advisable. For, firstly, these are seldom of such a kind as to lead to a lasting relation between the contracting parties; secondly, limitations directed to such engagements tend to disturb, far more hurtfully, the security of negotiations; and lastly, for many reasons, but chiefly with respect to the exercise of judgement and strength of character, it is well that the word once given should be irrevocably binding; so that such an obligation should never be removed except where this is really necessary, and that such a necessity does not occur in the case of a transfer of things, is evident from the consideration that however they may hinder certain manifestations of human activity, they seldom tend to weaken the force of energy itself. But with contracts which render personal performance a duty, or still more with those which produce proper personal relations, the case is wholly different. With these, coercion operates hurtfully on man's noblest powers; and since the success of the pursuit itself which is to be conducted in accordance with the contract, is more or less dependent on the continuing consent of the parties, a limitation of such a kind is in them productive of less serious injury. When therefore such a personal relation arises from the contract as not only to require certain single actions, but, in the strictest sense, to affect the person, and influence the whole manner of his existence; where that which is done or left undone is in the closest dependence on internal sensations; the option of separation should always remain open, and the step itself should not require any extenuating reasons. Thus it is with matrimony.

Where the relation is indeed less intimate, while the personal liberty is still narrowly restricted, I am of opinion that the State should fix a time (the length of which must be determined by the importance of the restriction on the one hand, and on the other by the nature of the pursuit) during which none of the parties should be allowed to detach themselves without mutual consent; but that after its expiration, the contract, unless renewed, should not remain binding, even though the parties, in concluding the engagement, had abandoned the advantage to which such a law would entitle them. For although such a provision might seem to be nothing more than a boon of the law, and not to be *enforced* more than any other similar privilege, the course we suggest does not debar any one from entering into a lifelong contract, but guards against the possibility of constrained performance of an engagement, when such constraint would be injurious to the individual's highest aims. And indeed it is the less a mere boon in this, that the cases I have quoted, and especially matrimony (as soon as free-will no longer accompanies that relation), differ only in degree from that in which one party surrenders himself as a mere tool into the hands of others, or rather is made a tool by the other to further his designs; and the competence to determine generally in these the boundary between just and unjust constraint, cannot be refused to the State, that is, to the common will of society; since it would only be possible in special cases to decide accurately and truthfully where the limitation arising from a contract was such as actually to render him who has changed his wishes, a mere tool of the other. Lastly, it cannot be called imposing a boon, when we do away with the power of resigning it by anticipation.

The fundamental principles of right themselves establish it, and it has been already expressly laid down, that no one can make a valid contract, or, in general, enter into any engagement with regard to anything save that which is really his property, that is, his actions or his possessions. It is evident moreover that the chief solicitude of the State for the security of its citizens (in so far as this is affected by the operation of contracts or engagements), consists in watching and maintaining the observance of this principle. Still there are certain entire departments of transaction to which this fundamental rule has not been applied. Such, for example, are all dispositions of property to be observed after the death of the disposer, whether they be made directly or indirectly, incidentally in another contract or in a special contract or testament, or in any disposition of whatever nature. Right of any kind can only relate immediately to the person: its relation to things is only conceivable in so far as these are connected with the person by actions. With the decease of the person, therefore, this right is also at an end. Hence, as long as he lives, man is free to dispose of his things as he pleases, to alienate them in part or altogether—their substance, use, or possession; and further, to limit his actions and the employment of his means by anticipation, according as he thinks good. But he is in no respect entitled to define, in any way binding on others, what shall be done with his property after his decease, or to determine how its future possessor is to act or not. I will not here stay to examine the objections which may be urged against these positions. The reasons on both sides have been already sufficiently exhausted in the well-known question of the validity of testaments according to natural right ; and the point of right is, on the whole, of less importance in this case, as the competence of the whole society to attach that validity to testamentary dispositions which they would otherwise want, is clearly unquestionable. But as regards the practical extension afforded to testaments according to the system of our common law, (which, in this particular at least, unites the subtlety of the Roman jurisconsults with the love of power so eminently characteristic of the feudal system)—as regards this extension, they operate at once to restrict that freedom which is essential to human development, and so run counter to every principle we have unfolded. For they furnish the principal means through which one generation succeeds in prescribing laws to another—-through which abuses and prejudices, not likely otherwise to survive the causes which rendered their growth inevitable, or their existence indispensable, continue strong and living by inheritance, from century to century ; lastly, through which it comes, that instead of man giving their proper form and character to things, these latter, on the contrary, bring man under their subjection. Further, they divert man's views, beyond all else, from true power and its development, and direct them exclusively to external fortune and possessions ; since these are clearly the only means of securing obedience to their wishes after death. Finally, the arbitrary power of disposing property by testament is often, nay generally, made subservient to man's less worthy passions of pride, vanity, desire for dominion, etc., of which we are the more assured when we observe that it is not the best or wisest of men who avail themselves of this power : while the wise are not solicitous to arrange anything for a length of time, the individual circumstances of which they are too shortsighted to foresee, the good, so far from eagerly seeking for such opportunities, are too glad not to find an occasion which compels them to impose limits on the will of others. Too often, even, the considerations of secresy and of security against the censure of the world may induce men to make dispositions which otherwise very shame had suppressed. These reasons may serve to show the necessity of guarding against the dangers which may follow to the citizens from the practice of testamentary dispositions.

But what is to supply the place of such dispositions of property if (as principle strictly demands) the State were wholly to abolish the right of making them? As the necessary preservation of order and tranquillity precludes the possibility of any one taking possession, there clearly remains nothing but an hereditary succession *ab intestato* to be decided by the State. But to transfer to the political power such a mighty positive influence as it would acquire by the right of settling this hereditary succession, and by utterly abolishing the personal will of the ancestor, is forbidden by the principles we have already agreed upon. The close connection which subsists between laws on succession *ab intestato* with the political constitution of States has been frequently observed; and this source of influence might be employed to further other designs. On the whole, the manifold and ever-varying plans and wishes of individual men are to be preferred to the uniform and unchangeable will of the State. And we should remember, further, that whatever evils may flow from the practice of testamentary dispositions, it seems hard to deprive man of the innocent joy which attends the thought of continuing to do good with his means even after death; and although this feeling, it is true, begets an excessive solicitude for property, when too much encouraged, the utter absence of it might lead perhaps to the opposite evil. The liberty too, which men enjoy, of leaving their means behind them according to their own free disposal, creates a new bond of union among them, which, though often the source of abuse, may yet be attended with the happiest results. And indeed the whole tenour of the ideas and arguments unfolded in this essay might fairly be reduced to this, that while they would break all social fetters asunder, they discover a thousand new and closer ties to reunite the web of human union, with the force of far deeper and more lasting sympathies. He who is isolated is no more able to develope himself than he who is bound by enthralling fetters. Lastly, it differs little whether a man really gives away what belongs to him at the very hour of death, or bequeaths it by will; and to the former he has an undoubted and inalienable right.

The contradiction seemingly involved in the reasons here advanced on both sides of the question, is reconciled when we remember that the dispositions of a testament admit of two kinds of settlement:—1. Who shall be the next heir to the property bequeathed? 2. How is he to manage it; to whom it is to be willed in turn, and, in general, what is to be done with it for the future?—and when we perceive that all the disadvantages above enumerated apply exclusively to the latter determination, while all the contrasting advantages flow only from the former. For if the laws have only provided, by determining the portion due to his family* (as

* This restriction on the power of bequeathing property, although it remains in other nations, is no longer a part of the law of England. For the exact nature and history of this limitation, the reader is referred to Blackstone's Commentaries, book ii. ch. 32. Quoting Glanvil, he says that "by the common law, as it stood in the reign of Henry the Second, a man's goods were to be divided into three equal parts, of which one went to his heirs or lineal descendants, another to his wife, and the third was at his own disposal: or, if he died without a wife, he might then dispose of one moiety, and the other went to his children; and so, e converso, if he had no children the wife

indeed they must so determine), that no testator can be guilty of real wrong or injustice, it seems as if the mere kindly wish to gratify, even after death, would leave no especial danger to be apprehended. The principles, moreover, by which men are guided in such actions will evidently be much the same at any given time, and nearly universal in their application; and the frequency or rarity of testaments will, in any period, serve to show the legislator whether the order of succession *ab intestato* which he has introduced, be still appropriate or not. It might perhaps, then, be advisable to make a corresponding division of the State measures which relate to testaments, according to the twofold character of the objects we have noticed as embraced by them; that is, to allow every man, on the one hand, to determine who shall inherit his fortune after his death, subject only to the limitation as regards the portion due to his family, but to forbid him, on the other, to enjoin in any way whatever how it shall be managed or employed. Now it is certain that the first of these privileges, which we suppose to be allowed by the State, might be seriously abused, and made the very means of doing that which it would prohibit. But it should be the object of the legislator to endeavour to obviate this abuse by special and precise regulations. This is not the place to enter into a full exposition of this subject, but I may propose the following as convenient examples of

---

was entitled to one moiety, and he might bequeath the other; but if he died without either wife or issue, the whole was at his own disposal. The shares of the wife and children were called their *reasonable* parts; and the writ *de rationabili parte bonorum* was given to recover them." This right to the *rationabilis pars* still continues to be the general law of Scotland. By this a man's movables are divided into three parts:—1. The *Dead's part;* 2. The *widow's part*, or *jus relictæ;* 3. The *Bairns' part*, or *jus legitimum*, a phrase which approaches the German word 'Pflichttheil,' which I have been obliged to render by a paraphrase. (See Burton's 'Manual of the Law of Scotland;' *Private Law*, p. 105.) —Tr.

such regulations : that the heir, in order that he be really the heir, be marked out by no express condition to be fulfilled *after* the death of the testator; that the testator nominate only the next heir to his possessions and never a subsequent one, since by this process the liberty of the first would be restricted; that the testator have the power of appointing several heirs, but must do this in a direct way; that he be allowed to divide a thing according to its extent, but never with respect to the rights connected with it—as, for instance, substance and usufruct, etc. From these flow manifold inconveniences and limitations of freedom, as also from the idea connected with them, that the heir is the representative of the testator,—an idea which (like so many others which have since become so extremely important) is founded, I believe, on a formality of the Romans, and therefore on the necessarily imperfect arrangement of the juridical constitution of a people who were only in process of formation. But we shall be able to rid ourselves of all these false notions if we keep the position distinctly in view, that nothing further is to be granted to the testator than, at the most, to appoint his heir; and that the State, while it should assist the latter to secure possession when his appointment is valid, must not lend its aid to the enforcement of any disposition on the part of the testator extending beyond this.

In case no heir has been appointed by the dying person, the State must arrange an order of succession *ab intestato*. But it does not come within my present design to develope the principles on which such an arrangement should proceed, nor of those which relate to the portion always due to the testator's family : I will content myself with observing, that the State should not have scope afforded it for the furtherance of its own positive aims in these, as in the other regulations we have considered—as in maintaining the splendour and prosperity of families, or the opposite extreme, of dissipating large fortunes by increasing the number of inheritors; but that it must always act in accordance with ideas of right, which are restricted in this case to the limits of the former co-proprietorship in the testator's lifetime, and must thus give the first claim to the family, the next to the municipality*, etc.

Very closely connected with the subject of inheritance is the question as to how far contracts between living persons may be transmitted to their heirs. We shall find the answer to this question in the principle we have already established: this is, that a man during lifetime may restrict his actions and alienate his property just as he pleases, but is not allowed to limit the actions of his heir after his own death, or, under such circumstances to make any other disposition except such as would secure a valid succession to his property. Hence all those obligations must pass over to the heir and must be fulfilled towards him, which really include the transfer of a portion of the property, and which therefore have either lessened or augmented the means of the testator; but, on the other hand, none of those obligations remain which have either simply consisted in actions of the testator, or related solely to his person. But, even after having made these limitations, there still remains too great danger of entangling the descendants in relations which are binding, by means of contracts concluded in the lifetime of the testator. For rights can be alienated as well as separate lots of property, and such alienations must necessarily be binding on the heirs, who cannot come into any other position than that which has been held by the testator; and thus

---

* I have been much indebted in the above remarks to the speech of Mirabeau on this subject; and should have availed myself still further of his reasoning, had not he proceeded from a wholly different point of view from that adopted in this inquiry. (See 'Collection Complète des Travaux de M. Mirabeau l'Aîné à l'Assemblée Nationale,' tom. v. pp. 498–524.)

the several possession of divided rights in one and the same thing, invariably leads to oppressive personal relations. It might therefore be advisable, if not necessary, for the State to prohibit the extension of such contracts beyond the lifetime of the persons concluding them, or, at least, to facilitate the means for effecting a real division of property, where such a relation has once arisen. To enter into fuller details to be observed in such an arrangement, does not come within my present design; and this is the less necessary when I consider that it should not be based so much on general principles, as determined by single laws, having distinct reference to single contracts.

The less a man is induced to act otherwise than his wish suggests or his powers permit, the more favourable does his position as a member of a civil community become. If, in view of this truth (around which all the ideas advanced in this essay properly revolve), we cast a glance at the field of civil jurisprudence, there seems to me, among other important objects, one that especially claims attention; I mean those societies which we are accustomed to denote as *aggregate corporations*. As they are always characterized by a unity, independent of the number of members who compose them,—a unity which, with unimportant modifications, maintains itself through a long series of years,—they produce in the end all those hurtful consequences which have been observed to flow from the practice of testamentary dispositions. For although, with us, much of their hurtfulness proceeds from an arrangement not necessarily connected with their nature,—namely, the exclusive privileges now expressly accorded them by the State, and now tacitly sanctioned by custom, and from which they often become real political bodies,—still they are essentially calculated of themselves to introduce many inconveniences. But these only arise when the nature of their constitution either forces on all the members certain applications of the common means, or, at least, by the necessity for unanimity, allows the will of the majority to be fettered by that of the minority.   Still, unions and associations, so far from producing injurious consequences of themselves, are one of the surest and most appropriate means for promoting and accelerating human development. All that we should expect therefore from the State would be an arrangement, that every corporation or association should be regarded simply as a union of the constituent members at any given time; and hence, that all obstacles be removed which would prevent them deciding in any given case, on the application of their common means according to the majority.   It only remains to provide that those on whom the society really depends should be considered as members, and not those only who are connected with it as instruments and accessories,—a confusion which has often occurred, and especially in decisions on the rights of the clergy; where the rights of the clergy have sometimes been mistaken for those of the Church.

From the reasons I have brought forward I would therefore deduce the following principles :—

*Where man does not confine himself to the immediate province of his own powers and property, but performs actions relating directly to others, the solicitude for security imposes on the State the following duties :—*

1. As regards those actions which are done without, or against, the will of another, it must prohibit any wrong to the latter in the enjoyment of his powers or the possession of his property; further, should he have actually sustained injury in these respects, it must compel him who has committed the wrong to give redress, while it prevents the sufferer from wreaking his private revenge on the other, upon this or any other pretext.

2. Those actions which are undertaken with the free con-

sent of the second party must be confined within the same (and not narrower) restrictions, as those which have already been prescribed in the case of actions relating to the agent only.

3. If of those actions already specified there are some from which future rights and obligations arise between the parties (single or mutual engagements, contracts, etc.), the State must protect the right of enforcement where it depends on what has been agreed on with due capacity for deliberation, so long as it refers to objects within the disposal of the transferring party, and has been transferred with full power of decision; but this in no case where the latter conditions are wanting, or where a third person would be unjustly restricted without or against his will.

4. Even in the case of valid contracts, if such personal obligations, or, still more, such a continuing personal relation follows as is calculated to impose narrow restrictions on freedom, the State must facilitate a release from the contract, even against the will of one party, and always according to the degree of its hurtful limitations on internal development. Hence, in cases where the discharge of the duties arising from the relation is closely interwoven with the inner sensations, it must always grant the power of unconditional release; but wherever (the limitation still being somewhat narrow) this connection is not so intimate, it must allow the power of withdrawal after the lapse of a certain time, this time to be determined according to the importance of the limitation and the nature of the pursuit.

5. If any one is desirous of disposing of his fortune in the event of his death, it might be deemed advisable to allow him to appoint his immediate heir, but without any condition being appended to limit the inheritor's power of disposing of the fortune according to his views and wishes.

6. It is necessary however to prohibit all further disposi-

H

tions of this nature, to decide on some order of succession *ab intestato*, and to affix the portion due to the testator's family.

7. Although contracts concluded by living persons pass over to their heirs, and must be fulfilled towards them, inasmuch as they modify what is left behind, the State should not only prevent the further extension of this principle, but it would be expedient to limit certain single contracts which give rise to intimate and restrictive relations between the parties (as, for instance, the division of rights in one thing among several persons) to the period of life only; or, at least, to facilitate their dissolution by the heirs of one or the other party. For although the same reasons do not apply as in the previous case of personal relations, yet the will of the heirs is less free, and the continuance of the relation indefinitely long.

Should I have succeeded in fully conveying my views by the recapitulation of these principles, they will serve to point out the true course to be pursued in all those cases which relate to the provisions for security designed by civil legislation. It is for this reason, for instance, that I have omitted all mention, in this recapitulation, of those incorporate bodies to which I referred; since, according to the origin of such societies in testament or contract, they are to be judged of by the principles established with respect to these. I cannot help feeling, however, that the very number and variety of the cases which come under the head of civil law, forbid my priding myself on any presumed success in this design.

# CHAPTER XII.

ON THE SOLICITUDE OF THE STATE FOR SECURITY AS MANIFESTED IN THE JURIDICAL DECISION OF DISPUTES AMONG THE CITIZENS.

THAT on which the mutual security of the citizens chiefly depends is the entire transfer to the State of all that concerns the redress of wrongs. Along with this transfer the duty is imposed upon the State of securing to the citizens that which they could not obtain of themselves ; hence, of deciding on right where it comes under dispute, and further of protecting him on whose side the right is found to be.

In so doing the State simply takes the place of the citizens, without the admixture of any interest of its own. For security is never really violated when he who is wronged is willing, or has reasons, to waive his right of redress ; but only when he who suffers, or believes himself to suffer, wrong, will not patiently put up with it. Nay, even if ignorance or indolence should bring men to neglect their personal rights, the State should not interfere to counteract this of its own pleasure. It may be considered to have discharged its sufficient duty when it has not furnished occasion for such errors by obscure and complicated laws, or by such as have not been properly made known. These considerations also apply to all means adopted by the State to solve the exact question of right in cases where redress is sought. That is, it must not advance a single step further in its investigation into the true nature of the case, than accords with the wish of the parties concerned. Hence, the first principle of every judicial proceeding should be, never to institute a search to discover the truth absolutely and in itself, but only to conduct the inquiry in so far as it is required by the party who is entitled to demand the full investigation. But here too it is necessary to observe this further limitation: namely, that the State is not to yield to all wishes of the prosecutor, but only in so far as such relate to the settlement of the right contested, and suppose only the application of such means as, even without the political union, man might justly employ against his fellow-man; especially in cases which only involve a dispute of right between them, and in which there is no violation, or where this is not immediately evident. The State, or the third power called in to the dispute, must only seek to secure the application of these means, and provide for their efficiency. Hence arises the difference between civil and criminal proceedings, that in the former the last resource for eliciting the truth is the administration of the oath, while in the latter the State enjoys far greater liberty in investigation.

Since the judge, as examiner into questions of contested right, occupies a middle place, as it were, between the two parties, it is his duty to see that neither of these is disturbed in his plans for obtaining redress or even delayed by the other; and hence we come to the second principle, equally important with the first: to keep the conduct of the parties under special supervision during the progress of the suit, and to take care that, instead of answering its ultimate design, it does not actually lead away from or wholly counteract it. The most exact and consistent observance of these two principles would give us, I believe, the best system of legal proceeding. For if the importance of the latter principle is overlooked, there is too much scope afforded for the chicanery of the parties interested, and the negligence and egotism of the advocates : thus the lawsuits become complicated, protracted, and costly ; while the decisions are often warped and falsified, irrelevant to the object, and unsatisfactory to the persons interested. Nay, these disadvantages often increase the very frequency of juridical disputes, and tend to promote the spread of a litigious spirit. If, on the other hand, the first principle we have noticed is not observed, the proceedings become inquisitorial, the judge gets undue power into his hands, and is disposed to meddle in the minutest private affairs of the citizen. There are illustrations of both extremes in actual practice ; while experience corroborates our conclusions, and shows us that whereas the latter of these errors operates to restrict freedom too narrowly, and in opposition to principles of right, the former extreme we have described tends to endanger the security of property.

In order to discover the true state of right in the disputed question, the judge requires indications of it, or means of proof. Hence we gain a new point of view in regard to legislation when we consider that right does not become an actual validity until, when contested, it admits of proof before the judge. It is from this that the necessity arises for new laws of limitation—that is, for those which require certain characteristic marks to accompany transactions of business, in order that thereby their reality or validity may be determined. The necessity for laws of this nature invariably decreases as the juridical constitution becomes more perfect ; and this necessity is the greatest when, owing to a defective constitution, the greatest number of external signs are required to establish proof. Hence it is that we find in the most uncultivated nations, the greatest number of formalities. In order to establish a claim to a field among the Romans, it was at first necessary that both the

parties to the transaction should be present on the very
ground; then it was enough to carry a clod from it into
court; afterwards a few formal words were deemed sufficient;
and, at last, even these were dispensed with. In general,
and especially in the less enlightened nations, the juridical
constitution has exercised an important influence on legislation—an influence often far from being limited to mere
formalities. The Roman doctrine of pacts and contracts
occurs to me to supply the place of other examples; and
although it is a subject which has been but little examined
or explained as yet, it can hardly be regarded from any
other point of view than that suggested by the above considerations. To inquire into this influence on different systems of legislation in different times and nations, would not
only be useful in many important respects, but would be
especially valuable in this—that it would determine what
kind of enactments might be generally necessary, and what
were founded only on local and peculiar circumstances.

Even though it were possible, however, it might be scarcely
advisable to abolish all limitations of this nature. For,
firstly, there would be too great facility afforded for forgeries, such as the substitution of false documents, etc.; and
secondly, lawsuits would be multiplied, or, if this does not
perhaps appear to be itself an evil, there would be too frequent opportunities of disturbing the peace of others, by
kindling useless disputes. Now it is that very spirit of
contention which manifests itself in lawsuits, which (apart
from the loss of time, fortune, and equanimity it occasions
the citizen) operates most banefully on the character;
while to compensate for these evils, it is attended with no
useful consequences whatever. The disadvantage, on the
other hand, of too many formalities are the increased difficulty of transacting business and the restrictions imposed
on freedom, which are, in any relation, of critical import-

ance. Therefore, as regards these also, must the law endeavour to adopt a middle course—that is, it must never require formalities for any other object than to secure the validity of negotiations; they are not to be enjoined, even with this design, except where the particular circumstances are such as to render them necessary, where forgeries might be seriously apprehended without them, and the proof be difficult to establish; and, lastly, such regulations only should be prescribed respecting them, as do not imply too many difficulties for their observance, while all should be removed from cases in which the transactions would become not only more difficult, but even almost impossible.

The due consideration, therefore, of security on the one hand, and of freedom on the other, appears to conduct us to the following principles :—

1. One of the principal duties of the State is to investigate and settle the juridical disputes of its citizens. In these it takes the place of the parties interested, and the only object of it is to protect from unjust demands, on the one hand, and, on the other, to give to just ones that due weight and consideration which could not be gained for them by the citizens themselves, but in some way prejudicial to the public tranquillity. During the process of inquiry, therefore, it must consult the wishes of the parties, in so far as these are founded on the strictest principles of right, but must prevent either from exercising unjust means against the other.

2. The judge's decision in cases of contested right can only be arrived at with the aid of determinate marks or characteristics, legally appointed. From this arises the necessity for a new class of laws, namely, those which are designed to appoint certain characteristics for assuring the validity of transactions touching right. In framing such laws the legislator must be guided by these two objects

alone:—to provide sufficient means for the authentication of transactions respecting rights, and to facilitate the proof which is necessary in lawsuits; secondly, to be careful of running into the opposite extreme, of rendering negotiations too difficult, while he must never impose regulations in cases where they would almost amount to render operations impossible.

# CHAPTER XIII.

ON THE SOLICITUDE FOR SECURITY AS MANIFESTED IN THE PUNISHMENT OF TRANSGRESSIONS OF THE STATE'S LAWS.

THE last, and perhaps the most important, of the means adopted for preserving the security of the citizens, is the punishment of transgression of the State's laws; and, in pursuance of the plan I proposed to myself, it now becomes me to apply to this also the fundamental principles we have already agreed on. Now the first question which presents itself here is this: what are the actions which the State can punish and brand as crimes? The answer readily suggests itself from what we have before observed. For as the State is not allowed to propose any other end to its activity than the security of its subjects, it may not impose restrictions on any other actions than those which run counter to this ultimate object. But it also follows as clearly that all such actions deserve a just measure of punishment. For (seeing that they disturb and destroy that which is most essential to human enjoyment as well as development) not only is their hurtfulness too serious, that we should not resist their influence by every means consistent with the end and accordant with morality, but it follows, further, from the principles of right, that every one must suffer the punishment so far to invade the province of his own right as the crime he has committed has penetrated into that of the other. But to punish actions, on the contrary, which relate to the agent only, or which are done with the consent of the person

who is affected by them, is manifestly forbidden by the same
principles that do not allow of their limitation; and hence
none of the so-called carnal crimes (rape excepted), whether
creating offence or not, attempted suicide, etc. ought to be
punished, and even the taking away a man's life with his
own consent should be exempt from punishment, unless the
dangerous abuse of this exemption should seem to necessitate a criminal law.   Besides those laws which prohibit
immediate violations of the rights of others, there are still
others of a different kind which we have already partly discussed, and must now again consider.  Since, however, with
regard to the ultimate object we have prescribed to the
State, these laws (although only mediately) conduce to the
attainment of that design, State punishments can apply to
these in so far as this punishment is not implied in the
transgression itself; as, for instance, in the breach of the
prohibition of *fidei commissa*, the invalidity of the dispositions follows as a consequence.  This is the more necessary,
as there would otherwise be an utter want of coercive means
for securing due obedience to the laws.   From these considerations on the cases to which punishment is to be applied, I shall now proceed to consider the measure in which
it is to be inflicted.  I believe it to be impossible in general
reasoning, which has no absolute reference to any particular local circumstances, to prescribe its due measure even
within ample limits, or to fix on the point beyond which it
should never go.   Punishments must be evils which deter
and intimidate the criminals.   Now, their degrees must be
as infinitely varying as the difference of physical and moral
feeling, according to the difference of the zones and ages.
That which may be justly called cruelty in one case may be
positively demanded by necessity in another.  Thus much
alone is certain, that, the same efficiency being preserved,
the system of punishment becomes more perfect in pro-

portion as it becomes more mild. For not only are mild
punishments lesser evils of themselves, but they lead men
away from crime in a way the more worthy of human
nature. For the less bodily painful and terrible they are,
the more do they become so in a moral point of view;
while excessive physical suffering tends to lessen the sense
of shame in the sufferer himself, and, in the spectator,
that of indignation and censure. And from this we see
that mild punishments might be much more frequently
employed than at first sight would seem possible; since
they gain, on the other hand, a compensating moral weight
and efficiency in proportion to their mildness. The efficiency
of punishments depends entirely on the impression they
make respectively on the soul of the criminal; and we might
almost affirm that, in a regularly graduated series, it would
be indifferent where we might determine to pause as at the
highest degree, since the actual efficiency of a punishment
does not so much depend on its absolute nature, as on the
relative place it occupies on the scale of punishments, and
since that which the State declares to be the highest punishment is readily acknowledged to be such. I say we might
*almost* affirm; for this assertion would only hold good when
the punishments inflicted by the State were the only evils to
be dreaded by the citizen. But so far is this from being
the case, that often it is real evils which urge him actually
to the commission of crime; and hence the measure of the
highest punishment, and therefore of the punishments in
general, intended to counteract these evils, must be determined with reference to them as well. Now, where the
citizen enjoys such ample freedom as that which these pages
advise, he will live in greater comfort, his soul will become
more calm and composed, his imagination more beautiful,
and punishment will admit of much relaxation in severity,
while it loses none of its real force and efficiency. So true

it is that all things good and beneficent in themselves are so blended together in a wonderful harmony, that it is only necessary to introduce one of these elements, to realize the blessed influences which flow from all the others. The general conclusion, then, to be derived on this point I take to be this, that the highest punishment should be that which is the mildest possible, under existing local circumstances.

There is but one kind of punishment, I think, which should be wholly excluded, and that is the loss of honour, the brand of infamy. For a man's honour and the good opinion of his fellow-citizens, is something which lies wholly beyond the reach of the political power. At most, then, such a punishment must be reduced to this : that the State may deprive the criminal of the characteristic signs of its own esteem and confidence, and leave to others the option of doing this with impunity. However unquestionable its claim to such a right may be, and however duty may seem to demand its employing it, I nevertheless cannot but consider the general declaration of its intention to avail itself of such a privilege, as by no means advisable. For, firstly, it presupposes in the person punished in such a way, a certain persistency in wrong which is but rarely found in actual experience ; and, secondly, even in its mildest expression (or if it went no further than to declare a just want of confidence on the part of the State), it is always too indefinite not to create much abuse, and, if merely for consistency's sake, would often embrace more cases than might really be necessary. For the kinds of confidence that may be extended to a man are, according to different cases, so infinitely manifold in their nature, that I hardly know of any crime which would shut out the criminal from the whole of these at once. But there is always a general expression of mistrust in such cases, and the man of whom it would be remembered only on parallel occasions that he had transgressed any particular law, carries about with him at all times an air of suspicion. Now, how hard such a punishment must be, we know from the feeling so common to all, that without the confidence of one's fellow-men life itself ceases to be desirable. Moreover, many other difficulties present themselves when we look more closely at the way in which such a punishment shall be applied. Mistrust of honesty will always follow where the want of it has been manifested. Now, to what an infinity of cases such a punishment would have to be extended requires nothing to show. No less difficult is the question, as to how long the punishment shall last. Every justly-thinking man would undoubtedly wish to confine its operation to a certain period. But will the judge be able to contrive that one who has so long borne the load of his fellow-citizens' mistrust, may at once regain their confidence on the expiration of a certain day? Lastly, it does not agree with the principles which run through this essay, that the State should give a definite direction to the opinions of the citizens in any way whatever. According to my views, therefore, it would seem well for the State to confine itself to the exercise of this its incumbent duty, viz. to secure the citizens against persons open to suspicion; and hence, wherever such a step is necessary,—as, for instance, in official appointments, the acceptance of the testimony of witnesses as trustworthy, the approval of guardians, etc.,—to exclude those persons, by laws expressly enacted, who had committed certain crimes or subjected themselves to certain punishments: beyond this, the State should refrain from any general manifestation of mistrust or any deprivation of honour. In this case also it would be very easy to fix on some time beyond which such objections should cease to operate. For the rest, it is needless to show that the State always retains the right of acting on the sense of honour by degrading punishments. Neither is it neces-

sary for me to repeat (now that I am treating of the general
nature of punishments) that no punishment whatever must
be inflicted which would extend beyond the person of the
criminal to his children or relations. Justice and equity
alike proclaim against such a course; and even the cautious
expression observed in the otherwise excellent Prussian code,
where such a punishment occurs, is not sufficient to lessen
the severity necessarily inherent in the thing itself.*

Since the absolute measure of punishment does not admit
of any general determination, this is, on the other hand,
so much the more necessary as regards its relative degree.
That is, it becomes us to ascertain what the standard should
be, according to which the degree of punishment attaching
to different crimes should be determined. Now, it seems to
follow as a consequence of the principles we have developed,
that this standard can be no other than what is suggested
by the degree of disregard for others' rights manifested in
the crime; and this degree (in so far as we are not referring
to the application of any penal law to an individual criminal,
but to the general apportionment of punishment) must be
decided according to the nature of the right which is violated
by the crime. It seems, indeed, to be the simplest method
of determining this, to judge according to the degree of
difficulty or facility of opposing the incentives to the crime
in question; so that the amount of punishment should be
estimated according to the number of motives which urged
or deterred the criminal. But when this principle is rightly
understood, we find it to be identical with the one we have
just laid down. For in a well-organized State, where there
is nothing in the constitution itself which is calculated to
incite men to the commission of crime, there cannot properly
be any other cause for criminal transgression than this very
disregard for others' rights, which the impulses, inclinations,

* Thl. 2. tit. 20. § 95.

and passions prompting to crime make use of. But if this principle be otherwise interpreted; if it is supposed that severe punishments should always be opposed to crimes in proportion as circumstances of time and locality render them more frequent, or, still more (as in the case of so many police crimes), in proportion as, from their very nature, they are less impressively resisted by moral reasons, then the scale would be at once unjust and hurtful.

It would be unjust. For as it is exact to suppose the prevention of future injuries to be the end of all punishment,—at least in so far as never to allow a punishment to be inflicted with any other design,—so the necessity for the punished one to undergo the punishment arises strictly from this, that every one must submit to infringement of his own rights exactly in that proportion in which he has violated the rights of others. Not only without the political union, but also within it, does the obligation rest on this position. For to derive it from a mutual contract is not only useless, but is also attended with this difficulty,—that capital punishment, for example, which is clearly necessary at some times and in certain local circumstances, could not be justified with such a supposition, and that every criminal could escape his punishment if before undergoing it he separated himself from the social contract; as we see, for instance, in the voluntary exile of the ancient republics, which however, if my memory does not mislead me, was only admitted in cases of political and not private crimes. To him, therefore, who has inflicted the injury, no discussion as regards the efficiency of the punishment can be allowed; and, however certain that the party injured would have no new injury to apprehend from him, he must still acknowledge the justice of the punishment. But it follows also, on the other hand, from this same principle, that he may justly resist every punishment exceeding the measure of his crime, however cer-

tain it might be that this punishment alone, and no milder
one whatever, would be efficacious.   There is manifestly an
intimate connection in human ideas between the internal feeling of right and the enjoyment of external happiness, and
the former seems to man to entitle him to the latter.   Whether this expectation is justified by the happiness which fate
accords him, is a more doubtful question, but cannot be discussed in this place.   But with respect to that enjoyment
which others can arbitrarily give or take away from him, his
right to it must perforce be acknowledged, while however
that principle seems *de facto* to deny it.

But, further, this scale is hurtful even to security itself.
For although it may enforce obedience to this or that particular law, it disturbs and confuses precisely that which is
the mainstay of the security of the citizens in a State, viz.
the feeling of morality, in causing a struggle between the
treatment a criminal meets with, and his own consciousness
of his guilt.   The only sure and infallible means of preventing crime is to secure a due regard to the rights of others;
and this object is never gained unless every one who attacks
those rights is in the same measure hindered in the exercise
of his own.   For it is only by such a correspondency that
harmony is preserved between man's internal moral development and the success of political arrangements, without
which even the most artificial legislation will always fail in
its end.   How much the attainment of all other objects
which man proposes to his endeavours, would suffer from
the adoption of such a scale as that to which we referred—
how much it contradicts all the principles laid down in this
essay, it is needless for me to show.   Again, the equality or
correspondency between crime and punishment which is demanded by the reasons we have developed, cannot be absolutely determined; we cannot decide in a general way that
this or that crime is just deserving of this or that particular

punishment. It is only in a series of crimes differing as to degree, that the means of securing this equality can be described; and in this case the respective punishments must be arranged in corresponding gradations. When, therefore, according to what we before observed, the absolute measure of punishment (for instance, of the highest punishment) is to be determined according to the amount of evil done, and that which is required to prevent the future commission of the crime, the relative measure of the others (when the highest, or indeed any, punishment has once been fixed) must be determined according to the degree in which the respective crimes are greater or less than that which it was designed to prevent by the first punishment decided on. The most severe punishments, therefore, should be allotted to those crimes which really infringe on the rights of others, and the milder ones to transgressions of those laws which are simply designed to *prevent* such infringements, however important and necessary those laws may be of themselves. By such a course the idea is at the same time banished from the minds of the citizens that they are treated arbitrarily by the State, and that its conduct towards them is not grounded on proper motives—a prejudice easily engendered where severe punishments are inflicted on actions which either really have only a remote influence on security, or whose connection with the latter is less easy to understand. Among the crimes first mentioned, those must be visited with the severest punishment which attack directly the rights of the State itself; since he who shows no regard for the rights of the State, shows that he does not respect those of his fellow-citizens, whose security depends upon the integrity of the former.

When crimes and punishments are thus generally apportioned by the law, the penal enactments so determined must be applied to single crimes. With regard to this application, the strict principles of right decide that the punishment can only affect the criminal in the degree of design or guilt implied in the action he has committed. But when it is agreed to follow out the exact principle before stated,—that in all cases the disregard manifested for the rights of others, and this only, is to be punished,—it must also be applied to single specified crimes. As regards every crime committed, therefore, the judge must endeavour to inquire carefully into the design of the criminal, and must have the legal power secured to him, of still modifying the general punishment according to the particular degree in which the criminal has disregarded the right violated.

The proceedings with regard to the criminal, moreover, are as clearly prescribed by the general principles of right, as in the way we have before adopted. That is, the judge must avail himself of all rightful means for discovering the truth, but must refrain from making use of any which lie beyond the boundary of legitimate right. He must therefore draw a careful distinction between the citizen who is only suspected, and the criminal who is actually convicted, never treating the former like the latter ; and, in fine, must never deprive even the convicted criminal of the enjoyment of his rights as a man and as a citizen, since he cannot lose the former but with his life, and the latter only by a legal, judicial exclusion from the political union. The use of such means, therefore, as imply actual deceit, should be as unlawful for this purpose as the employment of torture. For although it might perhaps be urged, in excuse, that the suspected person, or at least the criminal, authorized such a course by the character of his own actions, it is still wholly unbecoming the dignity of the State, which is represented by the judge ; and as to the salutary effects of an open and straightforward conduct even towards the criminals, it is not only evident of itself, but also in the experience of those

States (England, for example) which enjoy in this respect a noble and high-minded legislature.

It becomes necessary to examine, in the last place (now that we are treating of criminal law), a question that has assumed a high degree of importance by the efforts of modern legislation; the question, namely, as to how far the State is entitled or obliged to prevent crimes uncommitted. There is perhaps no public project which is animated by such a philanthropic design, and the sympathy which it inspires in every man of feeling is somewhat dangerous to the impartiality of the inquiry. Nevertheless, I cannot but consider such an inquiry especially necessary, since, if we consider the infinite variety of internal impulses from which the design of committing crime may proceed, it seems to me impossible to devise any method of wholly preventing such designs, and not only this, but actually hazardous to freedom, to prevent their execution. As I have already endeavoured to define the right of the State to limit the actions of individual men, I might seem to have already furnished an answer to this question. But when I found reason to determine, in that part of my inquiry, that the State should restrict those actions whose consequences might endanger the rights of others, I understood by these, (as the reasons I advanced in support of this position may show) such consequences as flow solely and of themselves from the action, and which might only be avoided perhaps by a greater amount of caution on the part of the agent. But when we speak of the prevention of crimes, we naturally mean the limitation of such actions only as give rise to a second, and that is, the commission of crime. Hence there is already this important difference, that the mind of the agent must here co-operate by a new decision; while in the former case it might either possess no influence whatever, or merely a negative one, by refraining from activity. This alone I trust will serve to show the limits with sufficient clearness.

Now all prevention of crime must be directed to its causes. But these causes, which are so infinitely varied, might be generally expressed perhaps as the feeling, not sufficiently resisted by reason, by the disproportion between the inclinations of the agent and the means in his power for gratifying them. Although it might be very difficult to determine it in detail, there would be, in general, two distinct cases of this disproportion; firstly, that in which it arises from a real excess of the inclinations, and, secondly, when it is a consequence of a deficiency of means even for an ordinary measure of inclination. Both cases however must be accompanied by a want of strong reasoning power and of moral feeling, which fails to prevent that disproportion from breaking out into illegal actions. Every effort of the State, then, to prevent crimes by suppressing their causes in the criminal, must, according to the difference noticed in these cases, be directed either towards changing and improving such positions of the citizens as may easily oblige them to commit crimes; or to limit such inclinations as usually lead to the transgression of the laws; or, merely, to gain greater force and efficiency for the arguments of reason and the operation of moral feeling. Lastly, too, there is another method of preventing crimes, viz. by legally diminishing the opportunities which facilitate their actual execution, or even encourage the outbreak of lawless inclinations. None of these different methods for effecting this object must be overlooked by us in the present inquiry.

The first of these, or that which is designed only to improve such circumstances as oblige the person to commit the crime, appears to be attended with by far the fewest disadvantages. It is of itself so beneficial, and calculated to enrich the means of power as well as of enjoyment; it does not immediately operate to restrict free activity; and although it is evident that all those consequences must be acknowledged to follow such a policy which I have before represented as the effects of the State solicitude for the physical welfare of the citizen, still they only follow here in a much smaller degree, since such a solicitude is extended only to a few persons. Nevertheless they do always really follow in the train of such a policy; the very struggle between internal morality and the external circumstances is done away with, and along with it its beneficial influence on the agent's strength of character, and on the mutual benevolence among the citizens in general; and the very circumstance that such a solicitude can only reach single persons, necessitates political interference in the individual circumstances of the citizens—all of which are injuries which we could only overlook in the conviction that the security of the State would suffer without some such arrangement. But there seems to me considerable room for doubt as to the existence of such a necessity. For in a State which does not give rise to such critical circumstances by the very nature of its own constitution, but which, on the contrary, secures such a degree of freedom to its citizens as that which it is the design of these pages to recommend, it is hardly possible in general that such situations as those we describe should arise, without finding a sufficient remedy in the voluntary assistance of the citizens themselves, and thereby rendering any State interference unnecessary; the cause in such a case must be looked for in the conduct of the man himself. But in this case it is wrong for the State to interpose itself, and disturb that order of events which the natural course of things induces in the man's actions. These situations, moreover, will only occur so rarely as to require no especial State interference, so that the advantages of such solicitude would be surpassed by those disadvantages which need no more detailed exposition here, after all we have already observed.

Exactly opposite in their nature to these we have adduced
in this case, are the reasons for and against the second
method adopted for the prevention of crimes—I mean that
which is designed to operate on men's very passions and inclinations. For, on the one hand, the necessity appears
greater in this case, as, when liberty is loosened from its
bonds, enjoyment becomes more wantonly extravagant, and
desires range more unrestrainedly; and these are tendencies
which the regard for others' rights, although it ever increases
with the sense of one's own freedom, might not perhaps be
sufficient to counteract. But, on the other hand, the disadvantage of such a policy increases in the very measure in
which the moral nature feels every fetter more deeply galling
than the physical. The reasons according to which it appears that any political effort directed to the moral improvement of the citizens is neither necessary nor advisable, I have
already endeavoured to unfold. Those very reasons apply
in this case in their full extent, and only with this difference,
that the State does not here aim at reforming morality in
general, but only at exercising an influence on the conduct
of particular individuals which seems to endanger the authority of the law. But by this very difference the sum of the
disadvantages increases. For, from the very reason that this
effort is not general in its operation, it must come short
of its proposed end, so that not even the partial good which
it realizes is sufficent to reconcile us to the injury which it
occasions; and further, it presupposes not only the interference of the State with regard to the citizen's private actions,
but also the power of influencing them,—a power which is
still more questionable when we consider those to whom it
may be entrusted. That is, there must be a superintending
power entrusted to persons either specially appointed, or to
the regular State functionaries who are already in office, over
the conduct and the situations arising out of it, either of all

the citizens, or of those who come under their immediate inspection. But in this way a new kind of domination is introduced, which is perhaps more oppressive than any other could be; and room is afforded for the indulgence of impertinent curiosity, bigoted intolerance, and even of hypocrisy and dissimulation. I hope I may not be accused of having endeavoured to picture abuses alone in this case. The abuses are here inseparably connected with the thing itself; and I venture to affirm that even though the laws should be the best and most philanthropic—should they allow to the superintending official nothing beyond the information to be gained through lawful channels, and the employment of advice and exhortation wholly free from coercion—and should the most perfect obedience be accorded to these laws, still such an institution would be at once useless and dangerous. Every citizen must be in a position to act without hindrance and just as he pleases, so long as he does not transgress the law; every one must have the right to maintain, in reply to every other, and even against all probability in so far as this can be judged of by another, "However closely I approach the danger of transgressing the law, yet will I not succumb." If he is deprived of this liberty, then is his right violated, and the cultivation of his faculties—the development of his individuality suffers. For the forms of morality and observance of law are infinitely different and varying; and if another person decides that such or such a course of conduct must lead to unlawful actions, he follows his own view, which, however just it may be, is still only the view of one man. But even supposing he were not mistaken in his judgment, —that the result even were such as to confirm its correctness, and that the other, yielding to coercion or following advice, without internal conviction, should not for this once transgress the law which otherwise he had transgressed,— still it would be better for the transgressor to feel for once the weight of punishment, and to gain the pure instruction of experience, than to escape, it is true, this one evil, but not to gain any greater clearness of ideas, or any active exercise of moral feeling; and it would be still better that one more transgression of the law should disturb tranquillity, and that the consequent punishment should serve as an instruction and warning, than that the very thing on which the tranquillity and security of the citizens depend,—the regard for others' rights,—be neither really greater in itself, nor now in this case be increased and promoted. Finally, moreover, such an institution cannot have the effect ascribed to it. As with all means which do not operate at once on the inner sources from which actions flow, it will only give another direction to the desires which run counter to the laws, and produce a dissimulation just doubly injurious. I have hitherto confined myself to the supposition that the persons to whom such a supervision as that of which we speak is entrusted do not produce conviction, but only operate through the medium of external arguments. It may seem that I am not authorized to proceed on such a supposition. But that it is well to exercise an influence on one's fellow-citizens and their morality through the medium of a living example and convincing persuasion, is too manifest to be expressly repeated. In any case, therefore, where such an institution produces these results, the foregoing reasoning cannot apply. Only it seems to me that to prescribe anything by law with a view to these ends, is not only unserviceable as a means, but even calculated to defeat the design in which it originates. For, firstly, it does not come within the proper province of the law to recommend virtues, but only to prescribe duties which can be enforced; and it will frequently happen that virtue will lose by such an attempt, since man only enjoys a course of virtuous action when it proceeds from his own free will. And, secondly, every mere request contained in a law, and every admonition or advice which a superior gives in virtue of it, is a positive command, which theoretically, it is true, men are not forced observe, but which in reality they always do obey. Lastly, we must take into account how many circumstances may oblige, and how many motives may incite, men to follow such advice, even wholly contrary to their convictions. Of this kind is usually the influence which the State exercises over those destined for the transaction of its affairs, and through whom it endeavours, at the same time, to operate on the other citizens. Since such persons are leagued with the State by special contracts, it is certain that it can exercise greater rights over them than over the other citizens. But if it faithfully adheres to the principles of the highest legal freedom, it will not seek to obtain more from them than the fulfilment of civic duties in general, and of those especial duties which are required by their especial offices. For it evidently exercises too vast a positive influence on the citizens in general when it tries to impose on these, in virtue of their special connection with it, anything which it has no right to impose directly on the other citizens. Without taking any positive steps in that direction, it is only too much anticipated by men's passions; and the task of preventing the evils which arise of themselves from these sources, will be amply sufficient to engross its zeal and vigilance.

A nearer motive for preventing crimes by the suppression of their exciting causes in the character is furnished by considerations of those who, by their actual transgressions of the law, awaken a reasonable anxiety with regard to their future conduct. It is with this view that the most enlightened modern legislators have endeavoured to make punishments at the same time reformatory in their operation. Now it is certain, not only that everything should be removed from the punishment of criminals at all calculated to do harm to their

I

morality, but also that every means of correcting their ideas and improving their feelings must be left open to them, so long as it does not counteract the object designed by the punishment. But instruction is not to be thrust even on the criminal; and while, by the very fact of its being enforced, it loses its usefulness and efficiency, such enforcement is also contrary to the rights of the criminal, who never can be compelled to anything save suffering the legal punishment.

There is still, however, a perfectly special case, where the accused party has too many reasons against him not to lead to a strong suspicion of his guilt, but still not enough to justify his being condemned (*absolutio ab instantiâ*).* To grant to him, under such circumstances, the full freedom enjoyed by citizens of good repute, is hardly compatible with the solicitude for security; and a constant surveillance of his future conduct hence becomes evidently necessary. The very reasons, however, which render every positive effort on the part of the State so questionable, and which recommend us in general to substitute the efforts of single citizens for its activity wherever this is possible, incline us in this case also to prefer the surveillance voluntarily practised by the citizens to the supervision of the State; and hence it might be better to allow suspected persons of this class to give security rather than to deliver them up to the surveillance of Government, which should only be exercised in cases where securities could not be obtained. We find examples of such security given (not in this case, it is true, but in similar ones) in the legislation of England.

The last method of preventing crimes is that which, with-

---

* According to the law of England, a man may not be tried twice for the same crime; and the plea of *autrefois acquit* is a bar to any indictment. But it has been the practice in some countries to suspend decision, as it were, where the guilt of the criminal is not sufficiently proved, and so leave it open to the prosecutors to renew the trial whenever more conclusive evidence is found,

out designing to operate on their causes in the citizen's character, endeavours only to prevent the actual commission of
them. This is the least immediately hurtful to freedom, as
it leads least of all to the exercise of any positive influence.
However, this method also admits of greater or less extension of its sphere and operation. For the State may content itself with exercising the most watchful vigilance on
every unlawful project, and defeating it before it has been
put into execution; or, advancing further, it may prohibit
actions which are harmless in themselves, but which tempt
to the commission of crime, or afford opportunities for re-
solving upon criminal actions. This latter policy, again, tends
to encroach on the liberty of the citizens; manifests a distrust on the part of the State which not only operates hurtfully on the character of the citizens, but goes to defeat the
very end in view; and is disapproved by the very reasons
which seemed to me to argue against the methods of preventing crime before-mentioned. All that the State may do,
without frustrating its own end, and without encroaching
on the freedom of its citizens, is, therefore, restricted to the
former course,—that is, the strictest surveillance of every
transgression of the law, either already committed or only
resolved on; and as this cannot properly be called preventing the causes of crime, I think I may safely assert that this
prevention of criminal actions is wholly foreign to the State's
proper sphere of activity. But only the more assiduously must
it endeavour to provide that no crime committed shall remain
undiscovered, and that no offence discovered shall escape un-
punished, or even punished more leniently than the law strictly
demands. For the conviction in the minds of the citizens,—
a conviction strengthened by unvarying experience,—that it
is impossible for them to infringe on the rights of others without suffering a proportionate loss of their own, seems to me
at once the only bulwark of internal security, and the only

infallible means of creating an inviolable regard for the rights
of others.   This is, at the same time, the only way to act
worthily on man's character, since we must not lead or compel him to certain actions, but only bring him to them by a
consideration of the consequences, which, according to the
nature of things, must flow inevitably from his conduct.
Hence, instead of all the more artificial and complicated
means for averting crime, I would never propose anything
but good and well-matured laws; punishments adapted, as
to their absolute measure, to local circumstances, and, as to
their relative degree, to the immorality of the crime; as
minute a search as possible into all actual transgressions of
law; and, lastly, the certainty of the punishment determined
by the judge, without any possibility of lightening its severity.   Should these means, so simple in their operation, be
somewhat slow in their effects, as I will not deny they may
be, they are, on the other hand, sure and infallible; they
do not hurtfully affect the freedom of the citizen, and they
exercise a salutary influence upon his character.   I need not
dwell longer on this subject, to point out the consequences of
the positions here laid down, as, for instance (a truth so often
observed), that the right of the sovereign to grant reprieve
or mitigation of the punishment cannot at all be allowed.
Such consequences are easily derived from the positions themselves.   The detail of arrangements to be adopted by the
State for the discovery of crimes actually committed, or for
the prevention of those which are only resolved upon, depends almost entirely on the individual circumstances of
particular situations.   We may only generally observe that
neither in this case must the political power transgress its
rights, and hence that it must not do anything contrary to
the freedom and domestic security of the citizens.   But it
may appoint proper officers to be on the watch in public
places where misdemeanors are most commonly committed;

establish public prosecutors, who may, in virtue of their office, proceed against suspected persons ; and, lastly, make it legally binding on all the citizens to lend their assistance to the task, by denouncing not only crimes which are contemplated but not yet committed, but those which are already perpetrated, and the criminal agents concerned in them. Only, in order not to exercise a hurtful influence on the character of the citizens, it must content itself with demanding the assistance last mentioned as the performance of a duty, and must not instigate them by rewards and benefits ; and in those cases where the fulfilment of such a duty would be impossible without breaking the nearest ties, it must wholly refrain from demanding it.

Lastly, before concluding this subject, I ought to observe that all criminal laws, as well those which fix the punishments as those which arrange the forms of proceeding, must be fully and clearly made known to all the citizens without distinction. I am well aware that a contrary practice has been repeatedly recommended, and the reason assigned for it is that no option should be afforded to the citizen of buying, as it were, the advantage gained by the unlawful action, with the evil of the punishment voluntarily undergone. But (even though we should for once allow the possibility of concealment) however immoral such a balancing of advantages would be in the man who would adopt it, still the State must not forbid it, nor indeed can any man forbid it to another. It has, I trust, been sufficiently shown, in what was said above, that no man is justified in injuring another, under the name of punishment, any further than he has himself suffered by the crime. If there were no legal determination of punishment, the criminal ought to expect about the same extent of injury as he would think equal to his crime ; and as this estimate would vary too much according to the variety of men's characters, it is very natural that a fixed measure

should be determined by law, and hence that there should
be a contract, not indeed to confirm the obligation to suffer
punishment, but to prevent the arbitrary trespass of all
limits in inflicting it.   Still more unjust does such concealment of the law become as regards the process of investigat-
ing and searching out crimes.   In this case it could evidently
serve no other purpose than that of exciting apprehension of
such means as the State even does not think fit to employ ;
and never should the State seek to act through fears, which
can depend on nothing else than the ignorance of the citizens as regards their rights, or distrust of its respect for
these.

I now proceed to derive, from the reasons here advanced,
the following ultimate principles of every general system of
criminal legislation : —

1. One of the chief means for preserving security is the
punishment of transgressions of the laws.   The State must
inflict punishment on every action which infringes on the
rights of the citizens, and (in so far as its legislation is
guided by this principle alone) every action in which the
transgression of one of its laws is implied.

2. The most severe punishment must be no other than
that which is the mildest possible, according to particular
circumstances of time and place.   From this all other punishments must be determined, in proportion to the disregard manifested for the rights of others in the crimes committed.   Hence, the severest punishment must be reserved
for him who has violated the most important right of the
State itself; one less severe must be inflicted on him who
has only violated an equally important right of an individual
citizen; and, lastly, one still milder must be applied to him
who has only transgressed a law designed to prevent such
injuries.

3. Criminal laws are to be applied to him only who has

transgressed them intentionally or culpably, and only in the degree in which the criminal thereby showed a disregard for the rights of others.

4. In the inquiry into crimes committed, the State may indeed employ every means consistent with the end, but none which would treat the citizen who is only suspected as already a criminal, neither any which would violate the rights of man and citizen (which the State must respect even in the criminal), or which would render the State guilty of an immoral action.

5. As regards especial arrangements for preventing crimes not yet committed, the State must only adopt them in so far as they avert the immediate perpetration. And all others, whether they are designed to counteract the causes of crime, or to prevent actions, harmless in themselves, but often leading to criminal offences, are wholly beyond the State's sphere of action. If there seems to be a contradiction between this principle and that laid down with regard to the actions of individual men, it must not be forgotten that the previous question was of such actions as in their immediate conse-quences were likely to infringe on the rights of others, and that here we are considering those from which, in order to produce this effect, a second action must arise. The con-cealment of pregnancy—to illustrate what I mean by an ex-ample—ought not to be forbidden in order to prevent infan-ticide (unless we were to regard it as already an indication of the mother's intention), but as an action which, of itself, and without any such intention, might be dangerous to the life of the infant.

# CHAPTER XIV.

## ON THE SOLICITUDE OF THE STATE FOR THE WELFARE OF MINORS, LUNATICS, AND IDIOTS.

ALL the principles I have hitherto endeavoured to establish in this essay, presuppose men to be in the full exercise of their ripened powers of understanding. For they are all grounded on the conviction, that the man who thinks and acts for himself should never be robbed of the power of voluntarily deciding on all that concerns himself, according to the results of his deliberations. Hence, then, they cannot be applied to persons such as lunatics and idiots, who are almost wholly deprived of reason, or to those in whom it has not reached that maturity which depends on the very growth and maturity of the body. For, however indefinite and, strictly speaking, incorrect, the latter standard may be, still there can be no other valid test to enable us to judge in general of others. Now, all these persons require, in the strictest sense, a positive solicitude for their physical and moral wellbeing, and the mere negative regard for their security is not enough to meet the wants of their peculiar position. But, to begin with children, who constitute the largest and most important class of such persons, it is evident that the care for their welfare, in virtue of the principles of right, peculiarly belongs to certain persons, that is, their parents. It is their duty to train up their offspring to perfect maturity; and from this duty, and as the necessary conditions of its exercise, flow all their rights with regard to them. The children, therefore, retain all their original rights as regards their life, their health, their fortune (if they already possess any), and should not be limited even in their freedom, except in so far as the parents may think necessary, partly for their own development, and partly to preserve the newly-arisen domestic relations, while such limitations should not extend beyond the time required for their training.  Children must never be compelled to actions which extend in their immediate consequences beyond this period of development, or even over the whole life.  Hence, for example, they cannot be bound in the matter of marriage, or be obliged to follow any particular career.  With the age of maturity the power of the parents must necessarily cease altogether.  The duty of the parents, then, may be thus generally defined,—to put their children in a condition (partly by personal care for their physical and moral well-being, and partly by providing them with the necessary means) to choose a plan of life for themselves, while they are only restricted in that choice by the circumstances of their individual position; the duty of the children, on the other hand, consists in doing all that is necessary for the sufficient performance of that duty on the part of the parents.  I shall not pause here to enumerate and examine in detail all that these respective duties comprehend.  Such an examination belongs rather to a theory of legislation, and even in such could hardly be fully presented, seeing that it depends in great measure on the special circumstances of individual positions.

Now, it clearly belongs to the State to provide for the security of the rights of children against parental encroachment; and hence to determine, first, a legal age of maturity. Now, this must naturally differ, not only according to the difference of the climate and the epoch in which they live, but also according to individual circumstances, and the greater or less degree of intellectual maturity required in them.  In addition to this, it must see that the parental

power does not exceed its just limits, and must always regard its exercise with a watchful eye. Still this supervision
must never seek to prescribe any positive rules for the
definite training and instruction of the children by their
parents, but must confine itself to the negative precautions
necessary for preserving in both, the due observance of those
mutual limits and relations assigned them by the law. It
would, therefore, appear to be neither just nor advisable to
require parents to be continually rendering account of their
conduct towards their children; they must be trusted not to
neglect the discharge of a duty which lies so near to their
hearts; and only in cases where actual neglect of this responsibility has occurred, or where it may be immediately
apprehended, has the State any right to intermeddle with
these domestic relations.

To whose care the superintendence of the children's training must fall, after the death of the parents, is not so clearly
determined by the principles of natural right. Hence, it
becomes the duty of the State to decide distinctly on which
of the kinsmen the guardianship is to devolve; or, if none
of these should be in a condition to undertake the discharge
of this duty, to declare how one of the other citizens may
be chosen for the trust. It must likewise determine what
are the necessary qualifications for guardianship. Since the
guardians appointed undertake all the duties which belonged
to the parents, they also enter on all their accompanying
rights; but as, in any case, they do not stand in so close a
relationship to their wards, they cannot lay claim to an equal
degree of confidence, and the State must therefore double
its vigilance with regard to the performance of their duties.
With guardians, therefore, it might be necessary to require
that a regular account should be given of the way in which
they discharge the important trust reposed in them. According to our former principles, it is well that the State should

exercise as little positive influence as possible, even through indirect means.   Hence, then, as far as agrees with its care for the security of the children, it must facilitate the choice of a guardian by the dying parents themselves, or by the surviving relatives, or by the municipality to which the children belong.   And it should be observed further, that it is well to transfer the supervision of all special precautions to be taken in such cases to the respective municipalities; their measures will not only be always more exactly accommodated to the individual circumstances of the wards, but will be more various and less uniform in their character; and so long as the chief superintendence remains in the hands of the State itself, the security of the wards is sufficiently provided for.

In addition to these arrangements in the case of minors, the State should not rest satisfied with protecting them, like other citizens, from outward encroachment, but must advance a step further in this respect. It has been before laid down, that every man may dispose of his fortune or determine on his actions, according as the case may be, of his own free-will.   Such freedom might be dangerous, in more respects than one, to persons whose judgment was not fully matured. It is, indeed, the duty of the parents, or of the guardians, to whom the superintendence of the minor's actions is confided, to ward off such risks.   But the State must come in to aid them in this respect, and also consult the interests of the minors themselves, by declaring such of their actions void as are likely to be prejudicial to them in their consequences. It must thereby baffle the interested designs of others to deceive them and surprise them into false decisions.   Where such designs have succeeded, the State must not only enforce the reparation of the loss, but must also punish the parties to the deception; and thus actions may become punishable which would otherwise be beyond the reach of legal control.

I may here mention illicit sexual intercourse as an example; in which, according to these principles, the State must punish in the person of the perpetrator, when the offence has been committed with a minor. But as human actions require infinitely different degrees of judgment, and the latter only reaches its maturity by successive stages, it is well to fix on different times and degrees of minority by which the validity of different actions may be determined.

What we have here observed respecting minors, applies also to the provisions to be made in the case of idiots and madmen. The difference chiefly consists in this, that these do not require education and training (unless we apply this name to the efforts made to restore them to the use of their reason), but only care and supervision; that in their case, moreover, it is principally the injury they might do to others which is to be prevented, and that they are generally in a condition which forbids the enjoyment either of their personal powers or fortunes. It is only necessary to observe, with regard to these, that as the return to reason is yet possible, the temporary exercise of their rights is all that should be taken from them, and not those rights themselves. As my present design does not permit me to enter more fully into the case of such persons, I shall conclude the subject with the statement of the following general principles :—

1. Those persons who are deprived of their proper powers of understanding, or have not yet reached the age necessary for the possession of them, require the exercise of a special solicitude towards them, as regards their physical, intellectual, and moral welfare. Persons of this kind are minors and those deprived of reason. First, of the former class; and, secondly, of the latter.

2. In the case of minors, the State must determine the duration of their minority. It must provide in this that the period be neither too long nor too short to be essentially hurt-

ful—deciding according to the individual circumstances of
the condition of the nation, and guided by considerations of
the period required for the full development of the body, as
an approximative characteristic.  It is advisable that certain
times should be appointed for the expiration of minority as
regards the validity of different actions, and that the freedom
of the minors be gradually enlarged while the supervision of
their affairs is proportionately diminished.

3. The State must see that the parents strictly fulfil their
duty towards their children, that is, to befit them, as far as
their situation allows, to choose a plan of life of their own;
and that the children, on their part, discharge the duty they
owe to their parents, that is, to do all to enable the latter to
fulfil their duty with regard to them; while neither parents
nor children be allowed to overstep the rights which the
discharge of their mutual duty puts into their hands.   To
secure this object alone must be the State's endeavour; and
every attempt to bring out positive ends through the pre-
tence of this solicitude,—as, for example, to encourage a particular development of the children's powers,—must be regarded as foreign to its appropriate sphere.

4. In the event of the death of the parents, guardians are
necessary to be appointed.  The State, therefore, should
determine the way in which they are to be chosen, and
the qualifications requisite in them for the proper performance of their trust.  But it will do well to provide that they
be appointed by the parents before their death, or by the
surviving relatives, or by the municipality to which the
minors belong.  The conduct of the guardian in the discharge of his duty requires especial supervision on the part
of the State.

5. In order to provide for the security of minors, and that
their inexperience and rashness be not employed by others
to prejudice their interests, the State must declare all such

actions void as have been ventured on by themselves, and
are likely to be hurtful to them in their consequences, and
must punish those who have availed themselves of the inexperience of the minors in this way.

6. All that is here said of minors applies likewise to those
who are deprived of reason, with the difference only which
is suggested by the nature of the thing itself. No one moreover should be regarded in such a condition until he has been
formally declared to be so, after an inquiry into the circumstances by medical men, and under the supervision of the
magistrate; and the evil itself must always be considered as
temporary, and the return of reason possible.

I have now considered all the objects to which State
agency should be directed, and have endeavoured to lay
down the ultimate principle by which it should be guided
in each. Should this essay appear imperfect, and should I
seem to have omitted much that is important in legislation,
it must not be forgotten that it was not my intention to con-
struct a theory of legislation (a task above my knowledge and
abilities), but only to make it clearly evident how far legislation in its different branches might extend or restrict the
limits of State agency. For, as legislation may be divided
according to its objects, it can also be arranged according
to its sources; and perhaps the latter system of division,
particularly as regards the legislator himself, is especially
interesting and rich in results. There seem to me to be only
three such sources, or, to speak more correctly, three grand
points of view from which the necessity of laws appears.
The general object of legislation is to determine all that concerns the actions of the citizen and their necessary consequences. The first point of view, therefore, arises from the
nature of those actions themselves, and of such of their consequences as flow solely from the principles of right. The
second point of view is the special end of the State, the

limits to which it designs to restrict, or the circuit to which it would extend, its agency. Lastly, the third point of view is suggested by the means which the State requires in order to preserve the political organism itself, and to render the attainment of its ends at all possible. Every conceivable law must properly originate in one of these three points of view; but none should be made and enacted without regard to all the three, and the one-sided view in which they have originated is an essential defect in too many laws. Now from this threefold aspect we have three preliminary essentials for every system of legislation. 1. A complete general theory of right. 2. A perfect exposition of the end which the State should propose itself, or what is, in fact, the same thing, an accurate definition of the limits within which it is to restrict its activity, or a representation of the especial ends which are actually pursued by this or that State union. 3. A theory of the means necessary for the existence of a State; and as these means are necessary partly for the sake of preserving internal cohesion, and partly in order to assure the possibility of action, a theory of political and of financial science, or, again, a representation of actual systems of politics and financial economy. In this general classification, which admits of various subdivisions, I would only observe that the first-mentioned alone is eternal and immutable as human nature itself, while the others allow of divers modifications. If, however, these modifications do not proceed from perfectly general considerations, derived from all these different aspects of legislation, but from accidental circumstances; if, for example, there exists in some State a fixed political system, and financial arrangements which are unchangeable, then the second division we have mentioned is very difficult to preserve entire, and often through this the first and most essential suffers. The reasons for very many political imperfections might certainly be traced to these and similar collisions.

Thus I hope to have sufficiently indicated what I proposed in this attempted exposition of the principles of legislation. But, even with these limitations, I am very far from flattering myself with any great success in my design. The correctness of the principles laid down may not admit of question, but there is doubtless much incompleteness in the attempt to support and accurately define them. Even to establish the most fundamental principle, and especially as regards such an end, it is necessary to enter into the most minute details. But it was not accordant with my plan to enter into these; and while I strove my best to body it forth in my own mind as the model for the little I wrote down, I could not but be conscious of a greater want of success in the representation. I must, therefore, rest satisfied with having pointed out rather what remains to be done, than sufficiently developed the whole subject in all its parts. Still I trust I have said enough to render the whole design of this essay clearer, or to show that the grand point to be kept in view by the State is the development of the powers of all its single citizens in their perfect individuality; that it must, therefore, pursue no other object than that which they cannot procure of themselves, viz. security; and that this is the only true and infallible means to connect, by a strong and enduring bond, things which at first sight appear to be contradictory—the aim of the State as a whole, and the collective aims of all its individual citizens.

# CHAPTER XV.

## MEANS FOR THE PRESERVATION OF THE STATE ORGANISM. COMPLETION OF THE THEORY.

ACCORDING to the plan I proposed to myself in a former chapter,* I have now completed such portions of the whole inquiry as remained to be examined, and have, therefore, given as full and accurate a solution of the great question before us as my ability would allow. I might fairly conclude my task, then, at this point, were it not incumbent on me to refer, before doing so, to one final consideration, which is of the greatest importance as regards the whole subject; I allude to the means which are necessary, not only to render the activity of the State possible, but even to secure existence to the political power.

In order to accomplish even the most limited objects, it is evident that the State must be possessed of sufficient sources of revenue. My ignorance of all that is called finance prevents my entering here on an elaborate disquisition as regards that subject; but this is not to be regretted, seeing that such a discussion does not necessarily come within our present design. For, as I took occasion to observe in the outset, we are not supposing the case of a State whose objects are determined by the extent and efficiency of the means it may happen to possess, but rather that of one in which the latter are subordinate to and determined by the former. I have only to observe, for the sake of consistency, that it is no less our duty to regard, in financial arrangements also, the true end of man as member of the body politic,

* Chapter IX.

and the limitations naturally arising from such a connection. Even a moment's reflection on the close interdependence that subsists between police and financial regulations is sufficient to convince us of this. There are then, it seems to me, but three sources of State revenue :—1. The property which has been previously reserved for the State, or subsequently acquired; 2. Direct taxation; 3. Indirect taxation. The possession of any State property is attended with injurious consequences. I have already shown that the State must, by its very nature, obtain a preponderating power compared with private individuals; and in becoming proprietor, it must necessarily become mixed up with many private relations, while it preserves all its peculiar attributes. Now, it is the necessity for security which alone dictates the expediency of a political organization. But this necessity does not presuppose any particular division of property, or any determination of proprietors; and yet the State, in becoming proprietor, will extend all that influence to its interests of property, which has been granted for wholly different purposes, and will thus be able to outweigh all private individuals in this respect. Indirect taxation likewise is not free from hurtful consequences. Experience teaches us what a multiplicity of institutions is required to arrange and levy them; and of all these, according to our previous reasoning, we must unhesitatingly disapprove. Direct taxation, then, is all that remains. Now, of all the possible systems of direct taxation, the physiocratical* is unquestionably the simplest. But, as it has been frequently objected, one of the most natural products of all is overlooked

---

* According to this system, agriculture alone gives a clear profit or surplus over the yearly expenditure and original outlay, such as the cost of clearing, etc. Hence, agriculturists alone constitute the productive class; the other industrial classes are not productive; and between these come the landowners: the productive class creates the means of subsistence for the others and the material of their labour, and hence retains them in its service, as it were, for board and wages. Hence it follows that all impediments should be removed

in such a system; I mean human power, which, with our institutions, is also a disposable commodity, both in its working and results, and must therefore be subject likewise to direct taxation. If, however, the system of direct taxation (to which we are reduced) is not unjustly condemned as the worst and clumsiest of all financial systems, we must not forget that the government, whose activity we have so narrowly circumscribed, does not stand in need of such abundant sources of revenue, and that the State which has no peculiar interest of its own, apart from those of its citizens, will be more certainly assured of support from a free and therefore prosperous nation.

As the administration of financial affairs may create obstacles to the practical application of the principles we have urged, this is still more to be feared as regards the internal arrangements of the political constitution. That is, some means must be provided to connect the governing and governed classes of the nation together,—to secure the former in the possession of the power confided to them, and the latter in the enjoyment of what freedom remains after this necessary deduction. Different methods have been adopted in different States for this purpose : in some, it has been sought to strengthen the physical power of the government (a plan somewhat perilous for freedom); in others, the accomplishment of this end has been attempted by bringing contending and counterbalancing forces into opposition ; and in others, by diffusing throughout the nation a spirit favourable to the constitution. The last method we have

from agriculture, but also from industry and commerce, since in this way the unproductive expenditure is lessened and commodities become cheaper. In order, then, not to disturb industry and activity, the pure products alone should be taxed, and there should be but one tax, and that upon the land. See Quesnay's 'Tableau Economique,' 1758; Adam Smith's 'Wealth of Nations,' *passim ;* Hume's 'Essays and Treatises on Several Subjects,' London, 1753, vol. iv. p. 8, etc.

mentioned, although often productive of beautiful results (as we notice more especially in antiquity), has too hurtful a tendency on the individual development of the citizen, too easily induces one-sidedness in the national character, and is therefore most foreign to the system we have proposed. According to this, we should rather look for a constitution which should have the least possible positive or special influence on the character of the citizens, and would fill their hearts with nothing but the deepest regard for the rights of others, combined with the most enthusiastic love for their own liberty. I shall not here attempt to discover which constitution may be supposed to resemble this most faithfully. Such an investigation belongs evidently to a strict theory of politics; and I shall content myself with a few brief considerations, which may serve to show more clearly the possibility of such a constitution. The system I have proposed tends to strengthen and multiply the private interests of the citizen, and it may therefore seem calculated in that way to weaken the public interest. But it interweaves the two so closely together, that the latter seems rather to be based on the former; and especially so appears to the citizen, who wishes to be at once secure and free. Thus then, with such a system, that love for the constitution might be most surely preserved, which it is so often vainly sought to cultivate in the hearts of the citizens by artificial means. In this case of a State, moreover, in which the sphere of action is so narrow and limited, a less degree of power is necessary, and this requires proportionately less defence. Lastly, it follows of course, that, as power and enjoyment are often to be sacrificed on both sides to secure given results, in order to protect both from a greater loss, the same necessary accommodations are to be supposed in the system we have propounded.

I have now succeeded, then, in answering the question I

proposed myself, as far as my present powers would allow, and have traced out the sphere of political activity, and confined it within such limits as seemed to me most conducive and necessary to man's highest interests. In this endeavour I have invariably set out with a view to discover what was *best* in the several cases; although it might not be uninteresting to ascertain what course was most strictly accordant with the principles of *right*. But when a State union has once proposed to itself a certain aim, and has voluntarily prescribed certain limits to its activity, those ends and limits are naturally in accordance with right, so long as they are such that those who defined them were adequate to their important task. Where such an express determination of ends and limits has not been made, the State must naturally endeavour to bring its activity within the sphere which abstract theory prescribes, but must also be guided by the consideration of such obstacles, as, if overlooked, would lead to far more hurtful consequences. The nation can always demand the adoption of such a theory, in so far as these obstacles render it practicable, but no further. I have not hitherto taken these obstacles into consideration, but have contented myself with developing the pure and abstract theory. I have in general aimed at discovering the most favourable position which man can occupy as member of a political community. And it has appeared to me to be, that in which the most manifold individuality and the most original independence subsisted, with the most various and intimate union of a number of men—a problem which nothing but the most absolute liberty can ever hope to solve. To point out the possibility of a political organization which should fall as little short of this end as possible, and bring man nearer to such a position, has been my strict design in these pages, and has for some time been the subject of all my thoughts and researches. I shall be satisfied to have shown that this principle should be, at least, the guiding one in all political constitutions, and the system which is based upon it the high ideal of the legislator.

These ideas might have been forcibly illustrated by historical and statistical considerations, if both were directed to this end. On the whole there seems to me to be much need of reform in statistical science. Instead of giving us the mere data of area, population, wealth, and industry in a State, from which its real condition can never be fully and accurately determined, it should proceed from a consideration of the real state of the country and its inhabitants, and endeavour to convey the extent and nature of their active, passive, and enjoying powers, with such gradual modifications as these receive, either from the force of national union, or from the influence of the political organization. For the State constitution and the national union, however closely they may be interwoven with each other, should not be confounded together. While the State constitution, by the force of law, or custom, or its own preponderating power, imparts a definite relation to the citizens, there is still another which is wholly distinct from this—chosen of their own free-will, infinitely various, and in its nature ever-changing. And it is strictly this last,—the mutual freedom of activity among all the members of the nation,—which secures all those benefits for which men longed when they formed themselves into a society. The State constitution itself is strictly subordinate to this, as to the end for which it was chosen as a necessary means; and, since it is always attended with restrictions in freedom, as a necessary evil.

It has, therefore, been my secondary design in these pages to point out the fatal consequences which flow for human enjoyment, power, and character, from confounding the free activity of the nation with that which is enforced upon its members by the political constitution.

# CHAPTER XVI.

PRACTICAL APPLICATION OF THE THEORY PROPOSED.

EVERY development of truths which relate to human nature, and more especially its active manifestations, is attended with a wish to see worked out in practice what theory has shown us to be just and good. To man, whose mind is seldom satisfied with the calmly beneficent influence of abstract ideas, this desire is perfectly natural, and it increases in liveliness with the spirit of benevolent sympathy in social happiness and well-being. But, however natural in itself, and however noble in its origin, this desire has not unfrequently led to hurtful consequences,—nay, often to greater evils than the colder indifference, or (as from the very opposite cause the same effect may follow) the glowing enthusiasm, which, comparatively heedless of reality, delights only in the pure beauty of ideas. For no sooner has anything that is true struck deep root in human nature (even though it should be but in the heart of one man), than slowly and noiselessly it spreads its blessed influence over the surface of actual life; while, on the contrary, that which is at once transferred into living action, becomes not unfrequently changed and modified in its form, and does not even re-act at all on the ideas. Hence it is that there are some ideas which the wise would never attempt to realize in practice. Nay, reality is in no age sufficiently ripe for the reception of the most matured and beautiful thoughts; and before the soul of the artist, whatever his art may be, the fair image of the ideal must still hover like a model that is inapproachable. Such considerations, therefore, serve to point out the necessity of more than common prudence in the application of even the most consistent and generally accepted theory; and they urge it the more on me to examine, before concluding my task, as fully and at the same time as briefly as possible, how far the principles herein developed can be transferred into actual practice. This examination will, at the same time, serve to defend me from the charge of having thought to prescribe immediate rules to actual life in what I have said, or even to disapprove of all which contradicts the results of my reasoning in the real state of things,—a presumption I should be loath to entertain, even although I had sure grounds for supposing the system I have unfolded to be perfectly just and unquestionable.

In every remodelling of the present, the existing condition of things must be supplanted by a new one. Now every variety of circumstances in which men find themselves, every object which surrounds them, communicates a definite form and impress to their internal nature. This form is not such that it can change and adapt itself to any other a man may choose to receive; and the end is foiled, while the power is destroyed, when we attempt to impose upon that which is already stamped in the soul a form which disagrees with it. If we glance at the most important revolutions in history, we are at no loss to perceive that the greatest number of these originated in the periodical revolutions of the human mind. And we are still more strikingly convinced of this, when, on watching the influences that have most operated to change the world, we observe that those which accompany the exercise of human power have been the mightiest to alter and modify the existing order of things. For the influences of physical nature,—so calm and measured in their progression, and so uniformly revolving in their ever-returning cycles,—are less important in this respect; as are

also the influences of the brute creation, when we consider
these apart and of themselves. Human power can only
manifest itself in any one period, in one way, but it can
infinitely modify this manifestation; at any given epoch,
therefore, it betrays a single and one-sided aspect, but in a
series of different periods these combine to give the image
of a wonderful multiformity. Every preceding condition
of things is either the complete and sufficient cause of that
which succeeds it, or, at least, exercises such modifying influences that the external pressure of circumstances can produce no other. This very prior condition, then, and the
modifications it receives, act also to determine in what way
the new order of circumstances shall exercise an influence
on human nature; and the force of this determination is so
great, that these very circumstances are often wholly altered
by it. Hence it comes, that we might be justified in regarding
everything which is done on earth as both good and beneficial; since it is man's internal power which masters and
subdues everything to itself, of whatever nature it may be,
and because this internal power, in any of its manifestations,
can never act otherwise than beneficially, since each of these
operates in different measure to strengthen and develope it.
In view of this consideration, we understand how the whole
history of the human race could perhaps be represented
merely as a natural result of the revolutions of human
power; and while the study of history in this light would
be perhaps more pregnant than any other in interest and
instruction, it would at the same time point out to him who
designs to act upon his fellow-men, the way in which he
should attempt to sway and guide human forces successfully,
and the direction in which he must never expect them to go.
While, therefore, this human power deserves our especial
regard, commanding our respect and admiration as it does
by its precious and intrinsic worth, it has double claims on

K

our consideration when we recognize the mighty influence with which it subjects all other things to its sway.

Whoever, then, would attempt the difficult task of interweaving, artificially, a new condition of things with that which is already existing, should never lose sight of this all-important agency. He must wait, therefore, in the first place, for the full working out of the present in men's minds; should he rashly attempt to cut through the difficulty, he might succeed, perhaps, in creating anew the external aspect of things, but never the inner disposition of human nature, which would surely re-manifest itself in everything new that had been forcibly imposed on it. It must not be supposed that in proportion as full scope is allowed to the influence of the present, men become more averse to any subsequent change. In human history, it is extremes which lie most closely together; and the condition of external things, if we leave it to continue its course, undisturbed by any counteracting agency, so far from strengthening and perpetuating itself, inevitably works out its ruin. This is not only proved by the experience of all ages, but is in strict accordance with human nature; for the active man never remains longer with one object than his energy finds in it sufficient scope and material for exercise, and hence he abandons it most quickly when he has been most uninterruptedly engaged on it; and as for the passive man, although it is true that a continuing pressure serves to blunt and enfeeble his powers, it causes him to feel, on the other hand, the stringent influence more keenly. Now, without directly altering the existing condition of things, it is possible to work upon the human mind and character, and give them a direction no more correspondent with that condition; and this it is precisely which he who is wise will endeavour to do. Only in this way is it possible to reproduce the new system in reality, just as it has been conceived in idea; and in every other method (setting aside the evils which arise from disturbing the natural order of human development) it is changed, modified, disfigured by the remaining influence of preceding systems, in the actual state of circumstances as well as in the minds of men. But if this obstacle be removed,—if the new condition of things which is resolved upon can succeed in working out its full influence, unimpeded by what was previously existing and by the circumstances of the present on which this has acted,—then must nothing further be allowed to stand in the way of the contemplated reform. The most general principles of the theory of all reform may therefore be reduced to these :—

1. We should never attempt to transfer purely theoretical principles into reality, before this latter, in its whole scope and tendency, offers no further obstacles to the manifestation of those consequences to which, without any intermixture of other influences, the principles arrived at would lead.

2. In order to bring about the transition from the condition of the present to another newly resolved on, every reform should be allowed to proceed as much as possible from men's minds and thoughts.

In my exposition of abstract theoretical principles in this Essay, I have always proceeded strictly from considerations of human nature ; I have not presupposed in this, moreover, any but the usual measure of power and capability, yet still I imagined man to exist in that state alone which is necessary and peculiar to his nature, and unfashioned by any determinate relation whatever. But we never find man thus : the circumstances amidst which he lives have in all cases already given him some or other determinate form. Whenever a State, therefore, contemplates extending or restricting its sphere of action, it must pay especial regard to this varying form which human nature assumes. Now, the misrelation between theory and reality, as regards this point of political administration, will in all cases consist (as may easily be foreseen) in an insufficient degree of freedom; and hence it might appear that the removal of existing bonds, would be at all times possible and at all times beneficial. But however true in itself such a supposition may be, it should not be forgotten that the very thing which cripples men's power on the one side, furnishes it on the other with the food and material of its activity. I have already observed, in the beginning of this Essay, that man is more disposed to domination than freedom; and a structure of dominion not only gladdens the eye of the master who rears and protects it, but even the meanest underworkers are uplifted by the thought that they are members of a majestic whole, which rises high above the life and strength of single generations. Wherever, then, there is still such a commanding spectacle to sway men's admiration, and we attempt to constrain man to act only in and for himself, only in the narrow circle of his own individual power, only for the brief space during which he lives, all living energy must slowly pine away, and lethargy and inaction ensue. It is true that this is the only way in which man can act on the most illimitable space and on the most imperishable duration, but at the same time he does not thus act immediately; he rather scatters vital and self-germinating seeds than erects structures which reveal at once the traces of his hand; and it requires a higher degree of culture to rejoice in an activity which only creates powers and leaves them to work out their own results, rather than in that which at once realizes and establishes them before our eyes. This degree of culture it is which shows the ripe moment for freedom. But the capacity for freedom which arises from such a degree of culture is nowhere to be found perfect and matured; and this perfection, I believe, is ever destined to remain beyond the reach of man's sensuous nature, which is always disposing him to cling to external objects.

What, then, would be the task of the statesman who should undertake such a reform? First, then, in every new step which is out of the course of things as they exist, he must be guided strictly by the precepts of abstract theory, except where there are circumstances in the present on which to try to graft it would be to frustrate wholly, or in part, the proper consequences of that theory. Secondly, he must allow all restrictions on freedom to remain untouched which are once rooted in the present, so long as men do not show by unmistakable signs that they regard them as enthralling bonds, that they feel their oppressive influence, that they are ripe for an increase of freedom in these respects; but when this is shown, he must immediately remove them. Finally, he must make men thus ripe for enlarged freedom by every possible means. This last duty is unquestionably the most important, and at the same time, as regards this system, the simplest. For by nothing is this ripeness and capacity for freedom so much promoted as by freedom itself. This truth, perhaps, may not be acknowledged by those who have so often made use of this want of capacity as a plea for the continuance of repressive influences. But it seems to me to follow unquestionably from the very nature of man. The incapacity for freedom can only arise from a want of moral and intellectual power; to elevate this power is the only way to counteract this want; but to do this presupposes the exercise of that power, and this exercise presupposes the freedom which awakens spontaneous activity. Only it is clear we cannot call it giving freedom, when fetters are unloosed which are not felt as such by him who wears them. But of no man on earth—however neglected by nature, and however degraded by circumstances—is this true of all the bonds which oppress and enthral him. Let us undo them one by one, as the feeling of freedom awakens in men's hearts, and we shall hasten progress at every step. There may still be great

K 2

difficulties in being able to recognize the symptoms of this awakening. But these do not lie in the theory so much as in its execution, which, it is evident, never admits of special rules, but in this case, as in every other, is the work of genius alone. Theoretically, I should thus endeavour to solve this confessedly intricate problem.

The legislator should keep two things constantly before his eyes:—1. The pure theory developed to its minutest details; 2. The particular condition of actual things which he designs to reform. He must command a view of the theory, not only in all its parts, and in its most careful and complete development, but must, further, never lose sight of the necessary consequences of each of its several principles, in their full extent, in their manifold inter-connection, and (where they cannot all be realized at once) in their mutual dependency on each other. It is no less his duty (although it is doubtless infinitely difficult) to acquaint himself with the actual condition of things, with the nature of all restrictive bonds which the State imposes on the citizens, and which these (under shelter of the political power) impose on each other, contrary to the abstract principles of the theory, and with all the consequences of these restrictions. He should now compare these two pictures with each other; and the time to transfer a theoretical principle into reality would be thus recognized, when it was shown by the comparison that after being transferred the principle would be unaltered, and would produce the results represented in the first picture; or when (if this coincidence should not be perfect) it might yet be anticipated that this difference and shortcoming would be removed, after reality had more closely approximated to theory. For this last-mentioned goal, this continual approximation, should never cease to attract the regard of the legislator.

There may seem to be something strange in the idea of

these imaginative representations, and it might be supposed
impossible to preserve the truthfulness of such pictures, and
still more to institute an exact comparison between them.
These objections are not without foundation; but they lose
much of their force when we remember that theory still
yearns for freedom only, while reality, in so far as it differs
from theory, is only characterized by coercion; that we do
not exchange coercion for freedom only because it is impossible, and that the reason for this impossibility can only be
found in one of these two considerations—either that man
or the condition in which things are is not yet adapted to
receive the freedom, which (in either case) frustrates the natural results without which we cannot conceive of existence,
not to say freedom; or that the latter (a consequence which
follows only from the first supposition, or the actual incapacity of man) does not produce those salutary effects with
which otherwise it is always attended.   Now we cannot
judge as regards either of these cases, without carefully
picturing the present to our minds, and the contemplated
change in its full extent, and instituting an exact comparison between their respective forms and issues.   The difficulty still further decreases when we reflect, that the State
itself is never in a position to introduce any important
change until it observes in the citizens themselves those
indications which show it to be necessary to remove their
fetters before these become heavy and oppressive; so that
the State only occupies the place of a spectator, and the
removal of restrictions on freedom, implying nothing more
than a calculation of possibility, is only to be guided by the
dictates of sheer necessity.   Lastly, it is scarcely needed to
observe, that we are alluding here to cases in which a change,
proceeding from the State, is not only physically but morally
possible, and which contain therefore no contradiction to
principles of right.   Only it is not to be forgotten, with re-

gard to this last condition, that natural and general right is
the sole true basis of all positive law; that therefore we
should always revert to that natural foundation ; and hence
that (to adduce a point of law which is, as it were, the source
of all the others) no one can at any time, or in any way,
obtain any right with regard to the powers or means of another against or without his will.

Under this supposition I would venture to lay down the
following principle :—

*With regard to the limits of its activity, the State should
endeavour to bring the actual condition of things as near to
the true and just principles of theory as this is possible, and
is not opposed by reasons of real necessity. Now, the possibility consists in this, that men are sufficiently ripe to receive
the freedom which theory always approves, and that this
freedom can succeed in producing those salutary consequences
which always accompany its unhindered operation. The other
consideration, or that of opposing necessity, reduces itself to
this : that freedom, if once granted, is not calculated to frustrate those results, without which not only all further progress, but even existence itself, is endangered. In both of these
cases the statesman's judgment must be formed from a careful comparison between the present condition of things, and
the contemplated change, and between their respective consequences.*

This principle proceeds absolutely from the application, in
this particular case, of the principle we before laid down with
regard to all methods of reform. For, as well when there is
an incapacity for greater freedom, as when the essential results we have referred to would suffer from the increase, the
real condition of things prevents the abstract principles of
theory from manifesting themselves in those consequences
which, without the intermixture of any foreign influence,
they would invariably produce. I shall not add anything

further as to the development of the principle I propose. I might, perhaps, go on to classify the possible positions which reality may assume, and illustrate the manner of its application to those. But in attempting this, I should only contradict my own principles; for I have observed, that every such application requires a commanding view of the whole and all its parts in their closest inter-connection, and such a whole can never be exhibited by any mere process of hypothesis.

If we add to this rule, which we have laid down for the practical guidance of the State, those laws which are imposed on it by the theory we previously developed, we shall conclude that its activity should always be left to be determined by necessity. For the theory we have advanced allows to it only the solicitude for security (since security alone is unattainable by the individual man, and hence this solicitude alone is necessary); and the practical rule we have proposed for the State's direction serves to bind it strictly to the observance of the theory, in so far as the condition of the present does not necessitate a departure from the course it prescribes. Thus, then, it is the *principle of necessity* towards which, as to their ultimate centre, all the ideas advanced in this essay immediately converge. In abstract theory the limits of this necessity are determined solely by considerations of man's proper nature as a human being; but in the application we have to regard, in addition, the individuality of man as he actually exists. This principle of necessity should, I think, prescribe the grand fundamental rule to which every effort to act on human beings and their manifold relations should be invariably conformed. For it is the only thing which conducts to certain and unquestionable results. The consideration of the *useful*, which might be opposed to it, does not admit of any true and unswerving decision. It presupposes calculations of probability, which (even setting aside the fact that, from their very nature, they cannot be free from error) always run the risk of being falsified by the minutest unforeseen circumstances ; while, on the other hand, that which is necessary urges the soul with an influence that is resistless, and whatever necessity demands is not only useful, but absolutely indispensable. The useful, moreover, since its degrees are as it were infinite, presupposes a constant succession of new arrangements and expedients ; while the limitations, on the contrary, which necessity enjoins, tend to lessen its very demands, since they leave ampler scope to the original power.   Lastly, the solicitude for the useful encourages for the most part the adoption of positive arrangements ; that for the necessary chiefly requires negative measures ; since, owing to the vigorous and elastic strength of man's original power, necessity does not often require anything save the removal of oppressive bonds.  From all these reasons (to which a more detailed analysis of the subject might add many more) it will be seen, that there is no other principle than this so perfectly accordant with the reverence we owe to the individuality of spontaneous beings, and with the solicitude for freedom which that reverence inspires.  Finally, the only infallible means of securing power and authority to laws, is to see that they originate in this principle alone. Many plans have been proposed to secure this great object ; to most it has appeared the surest method, to persuade the citizens that the laws are both good and useful.   But even although we admit that they possess these qualities in given cases, it is always difficult to convince men of the usefulness of an arrangement ; different points of view give different opinions ; and men are often prone to oppose convictions, and, however ready to embrace the utility of anything they have themselves recognized, to resist aught that is attempted to be thrust upon them.  But to the yoke of necessity every one willingly bows the head.  Still, wherever an actually complicated aspect of things presents itself, it is more difficult to discover exactly what is necessary; but by the very acknowledgment of the principle, the problem invariably becomes simpler and the solution easier.

I have now gone over the ground I marked out in the beginning of this Essay. I have felt myself animated throughout with a sense of the deepest respect for the inherent dignity of human nature, and for freedom, which is alone becoming that dignity. May the ideas I have advanced, and the expression I have lent to them, be not unworthy such a feeling!

THE END.

Made in the USA
Monee, IL
07 July 2022

99234076R00129